THE HUMAN CAPITAL
CONSULTING ROADMAP

FROM ASPIRING CONSULTANT
TO TRUSTED ADVISOR

DR. ANWESHA

Dedication

To my little brother,

Mentoring you on your journey into consulting reminded me why I fell in love with this field in the first place. Watching you find your path gave me the clarity and motivation to reflect, share, and ultimately write this book. This is as much yours as it is mine.

To Mum,

Thank you for always believing in me, even when I didn't. For lifting me up with your words, your strength, and your unconditional love. You taught me that my voice matters.

To Papa,

For your steadiness - thank you for showing me that patience and resilience are their own forms of brilliance.

To the husband,

You held it all together so I could chase my calling. Thank you for being my unwavering anchor, for handling everything else while I poured myself into these pages. I couldn't have done this without your support and love.

To Dobby, Dabbu, and my heartbeat **Dany**, my fur babies,

Your joy, loyalty, and unconditional love reminded me daily to pause, breathe, and keep going. Dany is no longer with us, but her spirit remains. "This one's for you too, baby girl—you are always with me, in every quiet moment, in every step forward."

To every aspiring human capital consultant who doesn't have a blueprint—this book is my way of saying: there is space for you here. **You belong.**

Acknowledgment

This book could not have come to life without the people and moments that shaped my journey.

To the clients who trusted me during their most complex and human moments of transformation—thank you for teaching me that real change begins with empathy.

To the mentors and peers who challenged my thinking, lifted me up, and encouraged me to share my story, your impact lives between these lines.

To the countless professionals, students, and early-career professionals who have asked questions, sought guidance, and shared their dreams, your curiosity is what built the foundation of this book. You are the future of this field.

To the team behind the Institute of Human Capital Practitioners (IHCP), thank you for believing in the vision of creating a space where human capital strategy is accessible, inclusive, and transformative. Your energy and commitment turned an idea into a platform and a platform into a movement.

And to anyone holding this book—thank you for investing in your journey. I hope these words serve not just as a guide, but as a companion as you find your voice in the world of human capital consulting.

About the Author

Dr. Anwesha is a human capital strategist, organizational consultant, and educator with over 15 years of experience guiding organizations through workforce transformation. Her career spans global strategy firms, Big 4 consulting, and senior leadership roles across industries, where she has enabled leaders to drive complex change, scale digital adoption, and implement future-ready talent strategies centered around people.

She holds a Ph.D. in Management, a Postgraduate Diploma in Training & Development, and an MBA. She is also a certified Project Management Professional (PMP) and a Prosci-certified Change Practitioner. Her expertise lies at the intersection of people, technology, and business strategy—helping organizations adapt to the rapidly evolving demands of work and the workforce.

As the Founder and CEO of the Institute for Human Capital Practitioners (IHCP), Dr. Anwesha leads a growing platform focused on education, thought leadership, and practitioner-level training in human capital consulting. IHCP bridges theory with application, equipping both aspiring and experienced consultants with the tools to lead meaningful workforce transformations. She also heads its consulting arm, DA Consulting & Advisory, through which she delivers large-scale transformation initiatives focused on leadership development, organizational change, enterprise learning, and HR technology adoption.

A dedicated mentor, Dr. Anwesha has supported hundreds of early-career professionals and career changers in breaking into consulting—championing a people-first approach rooted in empathy, intentionality, and impact.

Currently pursuing her second doctorate—a Doctorate in Business Administration (DBA) at the University of Calgary—her research explores how individuals and organizations can adapt to the future of work through transformational learning, strategic capability building, and mindset shifts. She is particularly focused on creating frameworks that help both people and institutions evolve in response to emerging technologies, shifting workforce expectations, and rapid organizational change.

A Canadian author of Indian origin, she brings a uniquely global lens to modern workforce challenges. When she's not working, you'll find her with a book in hand or spending time with her beloved dogs, Dobby and Dabbu.

This book is the culmination of her lifelong passion for people, learning, and purposeful change—a practical guide for anyone ready to build a meaningful and successful career in human capital consulting.

Table of Contents

Prologue

A Human Capital Consultant's Wake-Up Call: The Moment Everything Changed

"The rollout was supposed to streamline operations. Instead, half the team wants to quit. Can you fix this?"

The Vice President's voice was tight with frustration as she looked across the room. The leadership team sat in tense silence, their expressions a mix of exhaustion and desperation. The company had invested millions in a new digital transformation initiative, yet instead of boosting efficiency, it had sparked confusion, resistance, and declining morale.

As a human capital consultant, I had heard stories like this before, but now, sitting in that room, I felt the weight of the challenge firsthand. This was no longer about technical training modules or process optimization; this was about people. And if we did not act fast, the entire transformation would stall before it even had a chance to succeed.

I had seen it happen before. Organizations assume that if they design the perfect technology, structure, or business model, the people will automatically follow. But research paints a different picture, nearly 70% of change initiatives fail because they overlook the human side of transformation (Kotter, 1996). Without trust, engagement, and alignment, even the most sophisticated strategies fall apart.

It is not just about communication; it is about connection. People need to see themselves in the change. They need to understand the why, feel confident in the how, and believe in the who; they need leadership that walks the talk and embodies the change they are asking others to adopt. When this connection is missing, resistance becomes inevitable.

I knew then that my role was not just about HR policies, training, or change frameworks. It was about ensuring that employees felt heard, supported, and motivated to embrace what was coming. People do not resist change; they resist uncertainty, fear, and feeling like they have no say in what happens next.

This is the reason that real transformation starts with listening. Not just surveys and town halls, but active, empathetic engagement. Leaders must create space for honest dialogue, acknowledge discomfort, and co-create solutions with the very people who will be most impacted. Change cannot be something done *to* people, it must be done *with* them.

This is what makes human capital consulting both challenging and deeply rewarding. It is about standing at the intersection of business ambition and human behavior, ensuring that change is not just managed but truly adopted. It is about making transformation not just a leadership vision but a shared mission that employees believe in.

That day, I walked out of the boardroom with a plan, not just to fix the symptoms of resistance, but to shift the narrative. Because when companies truly win the hearts and minds of their workforce, they do not just implement change. They thrive because of it.

Introduction

Why Human Capital Consulting Matters

Organizations succeed or fail based on how well they manage their people. Businesses invest millions in technology, strategy, and operations, yet without the right talent, execution falters. Human Capital Consulting (human capital consulting) exists to bridge this gap. It ensures companies attract, develop, and retain top talent while aligning workforce strategies with business goals.

Research confirms that when people thrive, businesses thrive; for example, companies with highly engaged employees are about 21% more profitable. This demonstrates how a strong people strategy directly drives business performance (Gallup, 2020).

Similarly, organizations that invest in employee development see 11% greater profitability and are twice as likely to retain their employees (LinkedIn Learning Report, 2023). These numbers show a simple truth: people are not just resources. They are the engine behind sustainable growth.

The demand for human capital consulting has never been higher. Digital transformation, shifting employee expectations, and intense competition for talent have made human capital advisory services essential. CEOs and CHROs no longer see

HR as merely an administrative function; they recognize that workforce effectiveness drives financial outcomes.

Take, for instance, a global financial services firm undergoing a major cloud migration. While IT focused on system architecture and integration, human capital consultants were brought in to manage the people side of change like redefining roles, supporting reskilling initiatives, and aligning leadership communication. The beneficial result is a smoother rollout, reduced turnover, and faster adoption of new tools across the enterprise.

Human capital consultants lead initiatives that shape culture, implement workforce strategies, and optimize organizational design. They advise on everything from leadership development to change management, making them indispensable partners in business transformation. This aligns with industry findings that human capital concerns rank among the top challenges for CEOs—with leadership development, effective management teams, and succession planning cited as critical priorities (The Conference Board, 2015).

In a fast-scaling tech startup, for example, a human capital consultant might help founders formalize their talent strategy in defining performance metrics and compensation structures to building a culture that attracts high-performers. Without this guidance, the company risks growing faster than its people infrastructure can support, leading to burnout, misalignment, and costly turnover.

Companies turn to human capital consultants when facing complex workforce challenges. Mergers, acquisitions, restructuring, and new technology adoption create uncertainty and disruption. Organizations need experts who understand both strategy *and* people. Human capital consulting professionals help create clarity in times of change by conducting impact assessments, developing communication plans, and facilitating stakeholder alignment.

This growing reliance on human capital consulting professionals has made it one of the most sought-after careers in consulting. Industry trends reflect this demand; for instance, the human resource consulting market has been growing steadily in recent years. According to IBISWorld, the U.S. HR consulting industry alone is valued at over $25 billion, with projected annual growth driven by increased complexity in employment law, DEI initiatives, and remote workforce management. Those with the right skills can build a rewarding career in this field.

Human capital consulting operates at the core of three critical areas—at the intersection of Strategy, People, and Business Transformation:

Strategy: Organizations need the right workforce to achieve business objectives. Human capital consultants shape talent strategies, workforce planning, and leadership development to drive long-term success. For example, McKinsey's People & Organizational Performance practice helps businesses develop leadership pipelines, aligning talent with strategic growth. The logic is simple: without the right people in key roles, even the best business plans can fall short. Consider a global retailer entering a new market. Their success hinges not just on supply chain strategy but on having leaders who understand local dynamics, can build strong teams quickly, and adapt to changing customer expectations. Human capital consultants help ensure the right competencies are in place to execute the plan effectively. Moreover, strategic workforce planning is about anticipating future talents' needs according to the business forecast and industry trends. This is a proactive approach as it helps the companies in avoiding talent gaps that could derail growth.

People: Employees are a company's most valuable asset. A well-defined employee experience, a strong leadership pipeline, and a culture of continuous learning differentiate leading organizations from the rest. Research by Gallup underscores this, showing that companies with highly engaged workforces are significantly more productive and profitable. Human capital consultants focus on boosting engagement and building employee capabilities. They design initiatives like mentorship programs and career paths, knowing that engaged employees drive innovation and customer satisfaction.

Business Transformation: Every major change initiative depends on people. Whether it is implementing new technology, restructuring teams, or evolving workplace policies, human capital consultants ensure organizations navigate change effectively. Change management is often cited as a determining factor in project success—studies have famously shown that about 70% of change programs fail largely due to employee resistance and lack of support (Ewenstein et al., 2015). Skilled human capital consultants mitigate these risks by focusing on communication, training, and stakeholder buy-in during transformations. For instance, during an ERP system overhaul at a manufacturing company, human capital consultants led a cross-functional change network, delivered customized training modules, and created a feedback loop between employees and leadership. The initiative finished ahead of schedule, with minimal disruption and high adoption rates. In fact, projects with excellent change management are several times more likely to meet or exceed their objectives (Prosci, 2018). By helping manage the people side of change, human capital consulting experts make transformation efforts far more likely to succeed.

This work requires more than traditional HR knowledge. It demands business acumen, analytical thinking, and the ability to influence senior leaders. The best consultants connect workforce decisions to business outcomes, ensuring companies see a measurable impact from their talent strategies. They back recommendations with data—for instance, by showing that a new retention program reduced turnover by 25% or that a leadership training initiative increased employee engagement and productivity. Human capital consulting professionals operate with a blend of strategic insight and people-centric execution that drives real results.

Who This Book Is For

I wrote this book for professionals who want to build a career in human capital consulting. It will be especially useful for:

Human Resource (HR) Practitioners and Learning & Development(L&D) Specialists: Professionals seeking to elevate their work from operational HR or corporate L&D to strategic consulting, expanding their impact on business outcomes.

Business Professionals in Finance, Operations, and Marketing: Individuals who want to transition into people-focused consulting, leveraging their business knowledge in a new domain.

Experienced Professionals in Other Domains (IT, Strategy, Supply Chain): Project Managers, Analysts, or Client Management Specialists looking to pivot to human capital, applying their experience to workforce challenges.

Students and Early-Career Professionals: Those exploring opportunities in consulting and interested in the people side of business transformation.

Anyone Interested in Workforce Transformation: Professionals passionate about leadership development, organizational strategy, or shaping the future of work.

How to Use This Book

I have designed this book as a step-by-step guide to building your career in human capital consulting. Whether you are exploring the field for the first time or actively preparing for a transition, it follows a structured journey through four key parts. Each step is designed to equip you with the knowledge, tools, and strategies needed to succeed in this dynamic and growing profession.

Part 1: Understanding Human Capital Consulting – Learn the fundamentals of human capital consulting, key industry trends, and the core skills required. This section breaks down the various consulting domains—from Organizational Change Management to Workforce Transformation—giving you a clear picture of the landscape. By the end of **Part 1**, you will understand what human capital consulting truly entails and how it connects to broader business transformation efforts.

Part 2: Transferable Skills & Career Roadmaps – Discover how to leverage your existing experience and transition into consulting. **Part 2** identifies the key skills needed for human capital consulting and provides 90-day career roadmaps for professionals from different backgrounds. If you have ever wondered whether you have what it takes to break into consulting, this section will show you that you do— and it gives you the blueprint to make it happen.

Part 3: The Consulting Job Search & Career Acceleration – Learn how to craft a standout consulting resume, optimize your LinkedIn presence, network effectively, and ace consulting interviews. This section covers everything from personal branding to case interview preparation. Getting hired in consulting isn't just about having the right skills; it is about knowing how to position yourself. **Part 3** ensures you enter the job market with confidence and a clear strategy.

Part 4: Thriving as a Human Capital Consultant – Landing the role is just the beginning. Consulting is fast-paced and demanding. Part 4 offers guidance on how to manage multiple projects, deliver high-impact results, and carve a path toward long-term career growth once you are in the field. The goal isn't just to break into consulting—it is to thrive there. This section helps you build credibility, navigate common challenges, and grow into a top-performing consultant.

Each chapter includes exercises to assess your skills, case studies to illustrate key concepts, and practical tools to apply in real-world scenarios. By the end, you will have a clear path to enter and excel in human capital consulting. This book serves as both a career guide for aspiring consultants and a reference for professionals already working in the field which offers support and insight at every stage of the journey.

Human capital consulting offers the opportunity to shape the future of work. Companies depend on experts who can navigate workforce challenges and build high-performing organizations. If you are ready to step into this world, let's begin.

Part 1
Understanding Human
Capital Consulting

A Traditional HR Professional's First Consulting
Project: Bridging Experience with a New Mindset

"I have been in HR for 12 years, but I have never done consulting. What if I do not have what it takes?"

The words came from Maya, a seasoned HR Business Partner who had just joined our consulting team. She had spent over a decade managing HR operations, supporting business units, and implementing policies in a Fortune 500 company. But this was her first consulting project, and she was stepping into HR Technology (HRT) transformation, a world that felt unfamiliar and, at times, overwhelming.

Our client, a global financial services company, had engaged us to conduct a current-state assessment of their HR function and recommend a technology roadmap. The project required evaluating existing HR systems, identifying gaps in data processes, understanding the employee experience, and creating a solution for the future.

Maya was struggling to see how her HR background fit in.

"I know how HR works internally, but I have never advised a company from the outside. How is consulting different from what I used to do?" she asked.

I smiled because I had heard this concern before and had even felt it myself once. I explained, *"Consulting is not about having all the answers upfront. It is about asking the right questions, structuring the problem, and guiding the client to the best solution. Your HR experience is invaluable because you know what works in a real company. You just need to approach it from a strategic, problem-solving mindset."*

To help her transition, I broke it down into three key shifts.

HR professionals manage processes; consultants assess and optimize them – Instead of running payroll, recruitment, or performance reviews, consultants evaluate how effective these processes are and recommend improvements that could create real business value.

HR professionals execute; consultants advise – In her previous role, Maya implemented new HR software when corporate leadership decided to upgrade. In consulting, she would help clients select the right technology, build a strategy, and drive adoption before the implementation even began.

HR professionals know the "how"; consultants start with the "why." – Maya had been an expert in employee experience, HRIS systems, and talent management. Now, she needed to elevate her thinking and approach them like a business challenge: What problem are we solving? What outcomes matter to leadership?

For her first major task, she was responsible for interviewing HR leaders across the organization to assess pain points with their current HR technology. She came back from her first round of discussions energized:

"They are struggling with reporting across multiple systems. HR data is scattered, and managers cannot get real-time workforce insights. But I get it now; my job is not just to fix the process but to help them see what is possible."

In that particular moment, something changed. She was no longer looking at HR as a set of operational tasks, but as an ecosystem that could be redesigned, reimagined, and elevated through thoughtful strategy and collaboration.

By the end of the engagement, Maya had helped build a business case for a cloud-based HR transformation backed by real employee insights. She had not just learned consulting; she had realized that her HR background was her biggest strength.

"You do not have to start from scratch," I told her. *"You just need to see HR through a consultant's lens."*

Chapter 1: What Is Human Capital Consulting?

Organizations use different names for their team of human capital consultants—People Advisory, Workforce Transformation, People Consulting, People & Change, Talent Strategy, or Human Capital Solutions. Regardless of the name, the purpose remains the same—human capital consultants help organizations optimize workforce performance, align people strategies with business goals, and drive change. They ensure that a company's people practices; from hiring and development to engagement and retention—support its strategic objectives and bottom line.

The Role of a Human Capital Consultant: Human capital consultants operate at the intersection of business strategy and people management. Unlike traditional HR roles that often focus on routine operations or compliance, these consultants lead large-scale workforce transformations that directly enhance business performance. They act as strategic advisors who diagnose problems, design solutions, and guide organizations through complex implementation processes.

Consultants typically specialize in one or more areas within human capital, each requiring business acumen, analytical skills, and leadership.

Some of the key **specialty domains** include:

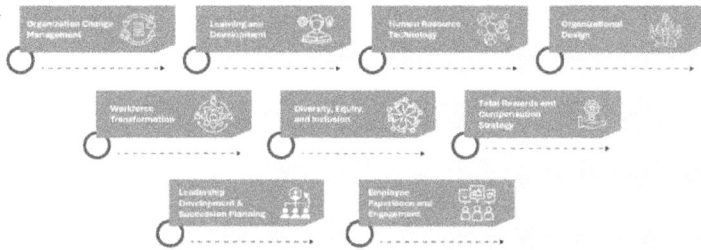

Organizational Change Management (OCM): Guiding companies through major transformations and ensuring employees adjust to change. This involves developing change strategies that mitigate resistance, crafting communication plans, and supporting leaders in driving the change. With effective change management, organizations can keep their business running smoothly during the transition. This is why, when implementing new technology or any other significant organizational change, it is important to avoid disruptions caused by frustrated users or support tickets.

For example, when a global bank adopted a new risk management system, it worked with a consulting team to train leaders, analyze employee readiness, and develop engagement strategies. This approach reduced employee resistance by 40%, illustrating how effective change management can significantly improve project outcomes.

Typical OCM tasks include identifying points of employee resistance during a change (for example, a new technology rollout), developing communication and training plans for restructurings, and creating readiness assessments to pinpoint risks in change adoption.

Why it matters: McKinsey research famously showed that ~70% of change programs fail to achieve their goals largely due to employee resistance and lack of management support (Ewenstein et al., 2015). Good change management can flip this script. Prosci's industry benchmarks indicate that initiatives with excellent change management are far more likely to meet objectives—up to six times more likely, in fact (Prosci, 2018). In other words, effective change management is often the deciding factor between transformation success and failure, not just a "nice to have."

Learning and Development (L&D): Designing and implementing employee training and leadership development programs that close skill gaps and prepare employees for future challenges. Companies depend on continuous learning to stay competitive, especially as technology evolves and new skills are required. L&D consultants might design competency frameworks, roll out learning platforms (like Workday Learning or Cornerstone), or create leadership programs for succession planning.

Example: Consider a manufacturing company struggling to adopt automation because employees lack the necessary technical skills. L&D consultants introduced targeted micro-learning modules to upskill employees into more technical roles, which reduced the need for layoffs by 30%. This showed how effective reskilling can benefit both employees and the business. In fact, a study by IBM found that new employees are 42% more likely to stay long-term at a company that invests in their training (IBM, 2014). This underscores how L&D efforts improve retention and protect companies from the high costs of turnover. Given that replacing an employee can cost anywhere from six months to two years' salary, investing in employee development is both a strategic and cost-effective move.

Human Resources Technology (HRT): Selecting, implementing, and optimizing HR technology systems (such as Workday, SAP SuccessFactors, or Oracle HCM) to improve HR processes and analytics. In today's data-driven environment, organizations rely on advanced HR systems to manage workforce data and derive insights. HRT consultants help companies choose the right tools, design new HR processes around those tools, and ensure successful adoption by end users. Their work includes assessing system requirements, mapping business processes to new platforms, and leading training for HR system adoption.

Why it matters: The integration of technology in HR is accelerating. Nearly half of companies have adopted AI in some capacity for talent or HR processes, and this number is growing. HRT consultants ensure that technology solutions align with business needs and that the organization can use them effectively. They also help harness people analytics; for example, using data from HR systems to forecast talent shortages or measure the impact of HR initiatives. This data-driven approach is essential. In one case, a consulting team identified through analytics that disengaged employees were four times more likely to leave within a year; armed with that insight, they helped an insurance company target interventions and reduced attrition by 15%. HRT consultants show how tech and data can be leveraged to solve people's challenges and demonstrate ROI on HR investments.

Organizational Design: Restructuring an organization's structure, roles, and processes to better meet strategic objectives. This could involve redefining job roles, clarifying reporting lines, or improving cross-functional collaboration. Consultants in this area assess business needs and develop new operating models to enhance efficiency and accountability.

Example: A retail company expanding into e-commerce found its traditional organizational structure was too siloed for the digital age. Human capital consultants redesigned the organization by introducing a new digital strategy team, consolidating redundant roles, and clarifying decision-making authority. The result was improved operational efficiency and a structure better suited to the company's strategy. Effective organizational design ensures that "structure follows strategy"; the organization is built in a way that enables its goals rather than hindering them.

Why it matters: As companies grow, adapt to market shifts, or adopt new technologies, outdated structures can slow them down. Misaligned roles, unclear decision rights, and siloed teams create inefficiencies and confusion. Organizational design consultants help untangle these issues by realigning structure with strategy, thereby improving agility, accountability, and collaboration. Research shows that organizations with clear roles and decision rights are 2.5 times more likely to outperform peers in total returns to shareholders (Worley & Williams, 2015; McKinsey, 2011). When structure supports strategy, companies move faster, make better decisions, and empower employees to focus on what matters most.

Workforce Transformation: Preparing organizations for the future of work by addressing workforce planning, reskilling, diversity and inclusion, and flexible work models. Consultants in this space help companies anticipate and respond to trends like automation, the gig economy, and remote/hybrid work. Their work focuses on strategic workforce planning (forecasting future talent needs), creating upskilling and reskilling programs, and implementing new ways of working (such as agile teams or hybrid work policies).

Case Example: A global retail company had high employee turnover and declining productivity. A human capital consulting team tackled the problem by: (1) conducting workforce analytics to pinpoint root causes of attrition (they discovered issues like limited career paths and heavy administrative burdens on managers); (2) designing a career progression framework and upskilling programs to improve retention; and (3) implementing digital tools to automate routine tasks, freeing managers to focus on coaching and strategy.

Impact: Turnover dropped by 25%, productivity increased by 18%, and both employee engagement and customer service improved. This illustrates how comprehensive workforce transformation efforts can directly boost business performance.

Diversity, Equity, and Inclusion (DEI): Developing strategies and programs that create inclusive and equitable workplaces. Consultants specializing in DEI help organizations build diverse teams and foster inclusive cultures. Their work might include conducting diversity audits, developing fair hiring and promotion practices, and rolling out unconscious bias training or inclusive leadership workshops.

DEI is increasingly recognized as essential for organizational success. Research shows companies with diverse leadership teams often outperform their peers financially, and a culture of inclusion helps attract and retain top talent. Consultants in this domain ensure that DEI isn't just a buzzword but is integrated into all aspects of talent strategy, from how job descriptions are written, to how performance evaluations are conducted, to how employees collaborate and voice ideas. By embedding diversity and inclusion into everyday processes, they help organizations unlock the full value of their workforce.

Example: A global professional services firm faced high attrition among underrepresented employees and lacked diversity in senior leadership. Human capital consultants conducted a DEI maturity assessment, analyzed attrition and promotion data by demographic segments, and facilitated focus groups to understand lived employee experiences. Based on the findings, they redesigned the performance review process to minimize bias, launched an inclusive leadership training for all people managers, and introduced a sponsorship program for high-potential diverse talent. Within a year, the firm saw a 20% improvement in retention rates among underrepresented groups and a measurable increase in internal promotions of diverse employees.

Why it matters: DEI is not only a moral and social imperative; it is a business one. Companies with diverse leadership teams are 36% more likely to outperform their peers in profitability, and inclusive workplaces are proven to boost innovation, engagement, and retention (McKinsey, 2020). Yet many organizations struggle to move beyond surface-level initiatives. DEI consultants bring a structured, data-informed approach to identifying systemic barriers and embedding equity into everyday practices. By shifting DEI from a one-off initiative to an integrated talent strategy, consultants help organizations unlock the full potential of every employee and build cultures where everyone can thrive.

Total Rewards and Compensation Strategy: Designing and implementing an effective rewards strategy is key to attracting, motivating, and retaining high-performing employees. This includes both financial compensation (base pay, bonuses, equity, etc.) and non-monetary elements (recognition programs, career development, flexible work options, and wellness benefits). Human capital consultants work with organizations to align rewards systems with business goals and employee expectations. A well-executed strategy not only supports performance but also reinforces organizational values and enhances employee engagement.

Typical consulting tasks include evaluating existing reward structures, benchmarking compensation against market trends, designing incentive plans, and ensuring pay equity across the organization.

Why it matters: Research from Mercer (2022) found that companies with holistic total rewards programs experienced 28% higher employee engagement scores. Moreover, non-monetary rewards have a greater long-term impact on retention when paired with meaningful career paths and transparent performance expectations.

Leadership Development & Succession Planning: Ensuring continuity in leadership is one of the most strategic investments an organization can make. Human capital consultants help organizations proactively identify, develop, and retain future leaders through structured succession planning and leadership development frameworks.

Succession planning goes beyond naming successors; it involves defining critical roles, assessing internal talent, creating development roadmaps, and preparing future leaders to step into key positions without disruption. Consultants also help integrate succession planning with broader talent, learning, and knowledge management systems.

Typical consulting tasks include designing competency frameworks, conducting leadership potential assessments, building development plans, and facilitating executive coaching programs.

Why it matters: According to Deloitte's 2023 Global Human Capital Trends report, only 16% of organizations say they have a strong leadership pipeline. A robust succession strategy reduces risk, improves retention of top talent, and sustains organizational performance during transitions.

Employee Experience and Engagement: The employee experience encompasses every interaction an individual has with an organization—from recruitment to exit. Engagement, a core element of this experience, reflects an employee's emotional and psychological connection to their work and the organization. Consultants support organizations in enhancing employee experience by conducting culture diagnostics, analyzing feedback data, and designing initiatives that address key engagement drivers like recognition, development, purpose, and well-being. The goal is to create a workplace where employees feel valued, supported, and aligned with the organization's mission.

Typical consulting tasks include designing employee journey maps, building engagement dashboards, facilitating listening sessions, and developing retention strategies.

Why it matters: According to the 2022–2023 SHRM State of the Workplace Report, 78% of HR professionals identified employee morale and engagement as a top priority. Gallup's

2023 workplace study further shows that highly engaged teams are 21% more profitable and 18% more productive than their peers.

Each of these specializations requires consultants to blend people expertise with strategic and analytical know-how. But beyond their specific domain, *all* human capital consultants share a common approach to their work, "a consulting mindset" that sets them apart from other HR professionals. The next chapter explores what that consulting mindset is and how it enables consultants to solve workforce problems differently.

Chapter 2: The Consulting Mindset

What Sets Consultants Apart: To excel in human capital consulting, it is not enough to be an HR expert or a "people person"—you must also learn to think like a consultant. This chapter explores how human capital consultants approach problems differently than traditional HR professionals, combining analytical rigor with strategic insight.

How Consultants Think: Consultants solve business problems through structured thinking, data-backed recommendations, and persuasive communication. While an HR practitioner might rely on personal experience or follow established policies, a consultant takes a more analytical, hypothesis-driven approach.

Here are some key aspects of the consulting mindset:

Structured Problem-Solving: Consultants break down complex workforce issues using structured frameworks (for example, the **MECE principle**—Mutually Exclusive, Collectively Exhaustive, to ensure clarity and completeness through analysis. By segmenting a problem into distinct components, they make sure no root cause is overlooked and, hence, craft targeted solutions.

Case Example: A consulting team supporting a healthcare provider's talent acquisition strategy faced broad hiring challenges. Using a structured approach, they separated the problem into three categories:

1) Internal mobility constraints (difficulty filling roles with internal candidates);

2) Inefficiencies in external hiring (slow recruitment processes and outdated employer branding);

3) Lack of predictive analytics for workforce planning (no data-driven forecasting for staffing needs).

By tackling each component separately, they could devise targeted solutions for each. This approach led to a 20% increase in hiring efficiency. The clarity provided by frameworks like MECE ensured that their solutions were comprehensive and addressed all parts of the problem. Consultants often borrow classic strategy consulting tools (like issue trees or 2x2 matrices) and apply them to HR challenges. The result is a clear roadmap of issues and actions—something especially valuable to business leaders who may not be HR experts themselves.

Data-Driven Insights: Modern consulting relies heavily on data and analytics. Rather than relying on assumptions or anecdotal evidence, human capital consultants use tools like employee surveys, HRIS analytics, and business intelligence software (for example, Power BI, Tableau, etc.) to derive actionable insights on workforce trends and behaviors. Instead of guessing *why* a problem is happening (say, high turnover or low engagement), they look at the evidence.

Case Example: In one case, a consulting team for an insurance company used employee engagement scores and exit data to demonstrate the risk to executives. A consultant might analyze data and reveal that disengaged employees are four times more likely to leave within 12 months. Armed with that insight, they convinced leadership to invest in a targeted leadership development program to re-engage employees. The result was a 15% reduction in attrition the following year. Similarly, data might show patterns like absenteeism spiking in certain departments or correlations between training hours and performance. Consultants turn these findings into action plans—for instance,

- Creating an analytics dashboard to flag high flight-risk employees.

- Implementing a new scheduling system to address absenteeism trends.

- Tailoring training initiatives based on performance data.

The key is that their recommendations are fact-based, lending credibility with analytical-minded executives.

Strategic Storytelling: Facts and analysis alone do not drive change; *how* you communicate them matters. Consultants are skilled at framing their insights as a compelling narrative that motivates action. One popular approach is the **Situation-Complication-Resolution (SCR) framework** for communicating a recommendation:

- **Situation:** What is the context or problem?

- **Complication:** Why is it urgent or tricky? What's at stake if nothing changes?

17

- **Resolution:** What should we do about it? (your recommendation)

Example: A consultant advising a logistics company on high warehouse staff turnover might present findings as follows:

- **Situation:** Turnover among warehouse employees is high (25% annually).

- **Complication:** This leads to increased recruitment costs and declining order fulfillment rates because new hires take time to train and aren't as efficient initially.

- **Resolution:** Implement structured career paths and pay progression to improve retention, giving employees a clear future with the company.

By packaging the recommendation in this SCR story format, the consultant helps executives quickly grasp why the issue matters and how the proposed solution addresses it. Storytelling in consulting often means using anecdotes, analogies, or simple visuals to make data meaningful. It is well known that stories "stick"—an executive might forget a statistic but remember a story of a frustrated employee that exemplified a broader trend. Combining narrative with numbers is a hallmark of effective consulting communication.

Moving from Task Execution to Advisory: A major mindset shift for professionals coming from corporate roles is moving from simply executing tasks to providing advice and proactive solutions. Consultants do not just do what they are told; they figure out what needs to be done, often before being asked, and then make it happen. They are the real problem solvers who anticipate needs, provide proactive guidance, and drive value beyond the immediate scope of work.

Imagine a corporate HR project manager rolling out a new HR software system—they might focus on tasks: scheduling training sessions, migrating data, and checking boxes. A human capital consultant, by contrast, will take a step back and zoom out to ask the bigger advisory questions:

- Why are we implementing this system?

- How do we ensure user adoption and ROI?

The consultant would possibly conduct stakeholder interviews to assess readiness, develop a change impact analysis to find potential risks, create an executive adoption roadmap, and set KPIs to measure post-implementation success. They frame each step as part of a larger goal, for example, ensuring the multimillion-dollar HRIS investment actually delivers long-term value. This proactive, advisory approach is what clients pay for. Clients have their own staff or internal teams to manage day-to-day tasks; they hire consultants for expertise, strategic thinking, and an outsider's perspective that connects the project to business outcomes. This proactive, advisory mindset is central to what makes human capital consultants indispensable.

Case Example: A financial services company rolling out a new CRM (Customer Relationship Management) platform didn't just need technical training manuals—they needed a holistic adoption strategy. A consultant tasked with this would:

- **Interview stakeholders** (salespeople, customer service reps, IT teams) to gauge readiness and identify concerns.

- **Analyze what could go wrong** – for example, risk of low adoption by certain groups or data not being entered correctly.

- **Develop mitigation strategies** for each risk (maybe a peer mentor system for less tech-savvy employees or a phased rollout plan).

- **Present a comprehensive plan** to leadership, linking each step to the ultimate objective: ensuring the CRM investment delivers a return (through high user adoption, quality data entry, improved sales processes, etc.).

This shifts the consultant's role from an implementer to a "trusted advisor and partner," which is crucial in consulting.

Delivering Findings with Impact: Finally, consultants are adept at delivering their findings and recommendations in a concise, impactful way tailored to different audiences. They know that a CEO, an HR director, and a frontline manager each care about different aspects of the same initiative. Typical consulting deliverables include:

- **Executive Summaries** – Concise, one-page overviews designed for senior leaders, focusing on high-level insights, recommendations, and expected ROI.

- **Change Impact Reports** – In-depth analyses that outline how transformation (like a merger, new system, or new technologies) will affect various employee groups, roles, and business processes.

- **Workforce Strategy Playbooks** – Step-by-step guides for HR teams to implement new strategies or programs (for example, a playbook for rolling out a new performance management system or DEI).

- **Capability Frameworks** – Strategic models outlining the skills and competencies needed for the future workforce, used for planning training or recruitment.

Case Example: A Deloitte consultant leading a workforce transformation project structured their final deliverables at three levels to align with different stakeholders' needs:

- A **C-Level Report** for executives, summarizing talent strategy insights and big-picture recommendations (the "why this matters" and ROI perspective).

- An **HR Execution Guide** for HR managers, detailing concrete steps to implement the changes (the "how to do it"—policies to update, communications to send, training to conduct).

- A **Workforce Planning Model** for analysts, providing a data tool with predictive insights for future hiring and retention (for continued analysis and monitoring).

By tailoring the message to each level of the organization, the consultant secured buy-in across the board and ensured the great ideas were actually executed effectively. This multi-tiered communication approach shows an understanding that CEOs, HR managers, and analysts all need information presented in different ways, even if it is about the same project. The best consultants pre-empt questions and concerns by delivering information in the format and depth each stakeholder prefers.

Consulting vs. Corporate HR Mindset – A Comparison: It is useful to contrast these mindsets directly. Suppose an issue arises: say, the sales department's attrition rate has spiked to 18% this year.

How might a typical HR manager approach it versus a human capital consultant?

An **HR Manager** might start by reviewing exit interviews for departing salespeople, consider adjusting the recruiting pipeline or salaries, or implement an engagement survey. These are all valuable, useful responses, but they tend to stay within the HR function and focus on process-level improvements.

A **Human Capital Consultant**, on the other hand, will frame it as a business problem and take a broader, structured, data-informed approach to drive positive outcomes, and they will:

- **Frame the problem in business terms:** How is high sales attrition affecting revenue or customer relationships? Are certain products or regions underperforming because sales positions are vacant?

- **Gather data:** Collect and analyze data—exit interview themes, employee engagement scores in the sales team, performance data, and manager feedback.

- **Segment the issue:** Is attrition especially high for certain roles (for example, account executives vs. sales support)? Certain regions or under particular managers? Identify patterns.

- **Form a hypothesis:** For example, "Mid-career salespeople are leaving because they see limited growth opportunities, so they jump to other companies for management roles."

- **Validate hypothesis with data:** Check if those leaving are mostly mid-level reps with 3 - 5 years' tenure and if their exit reasons align (lack of advancement, etc.). Conduct interviews with a few current employees for qualitative insight.

- **Craft a solution tied to business outcomes:** Perhaps create a **Sales Leadership Accelerator** program to provide a clear career path into management for top-performing sales reps, thereby increasing retention. Show how keeping these experienced reps will preserve customer relationships and avoid the ~$X million cost of hiring and ramping up new reps.

- **Present the case with a clear story:** "We are losing valuable salespeople at a high rate because they see no future here; it is costing us $Y annually in lost sales and increased hiring costs. We propose a targeted development and promotion program to retain them, which we project will save $Y and boost sales by $Z through better customer continuity."

Why it matters: This example illustrates the consulting mindset, the ability to think broadly and systematically and translating between HR and business language. The consultant approaches an HR issue (attrition) as a strategic business problem, uses data to derive insights, and proposes a solution that speaks to business value (money saved, revenue gained, risk reduced).

As you progress through this book—especially into **Part 2**—you will learn how to cultivate this consulting mindset even if your background isn't in consulting. It is a skill that can be practiced and learned, and it is essential for anyone looking to break into human capital consulting.

Part 2
Transferable Skills & Career Roadmaps

From MBA Graduate to Consultant: Bridging the Gap Between Theory and Practice

"I know the frameworks; I have studied the case studies, but how do I actually do this in the real world?"

The question came from Chad, a bright and ambitious MBA graduate who had just started as an intern in our consulting team. He had spent the last two years immersing himself in strategy, business analytics, and HR transformation models, but now, staring at his first client project, he felt completely lost.

"I understand the foundations of Human Capital Consulting," he admitted, *"but I do not know how to apply them. Everyone here seems to just... know what to do."*

I recognized the look in his eyes, the same uncertainty I had felt when I took my first steps into consulting. I knew that consulting is not just about knowing the theories; it is about applying them in real, high-pressure situations.

"You are not supposed to have all the answers yet," I reassured him. *"The key is learning how to think like a consultant—breaking problems down, structuring solutions, and asking the right questions."*

His first real assignment was with a retail client struggling with talent retention. Employee turnover was rising, and leadership wanted to know *why*. Chad immediately began pulling industry reports, referencing case studies, and researching best practices. But he was overwhelmed; he had all this information, yet no clear way to turn insights into action.

"What do I do first?" he asked.

I took him through a structured career transition roadmap—one that aligned his strengths with what consulting firms seek in top talent:

Step 1: Learn to Frame the Problem

I taught him how consultants structure issues using hypothesis-driven thinking.

Instead of looking for an answer first, we focused on asking the right questions:

- Is turnover highest in certain roles? Certain stores? Certain career levels?

- Is it compensation-driven, culture-driven, or growth-related?

- What data does the client already have, and what gaps exist?

Step 2: Translate Theory into Practical Consulting Deliverables

Instead of a lengthy research report, we outlined a three-slide executive summary with:

- One slide on key retention trends

- One slide on root cause hypotheses

- One slide on next steps and possible interventions

- This approach forced him to prioritize what mattered most, which is a critical consulting skill

Step 3: Strength-Based Career Roadmap

I asked Chad about his biggest strengths—he was data-savvy, great with visuals, and had a strong grasp of workforce analytics. So, instead of pushing him toward general HR consulting, I guided him toward HR Technology & People Analytics, where he could leverage his analytical skills.

The turning point came when we presented our initial findings to the client. Chad confidently explained how employee sentiment data revealed a disconnect between frontline employees and leadership—a key insight that leadership had overlooked.

After the meeting, he turned to me, grinning for the first time in weeks.

"I get it now. It is not just about knowing HR or business strategy; it is about thinking critically, structuring insights, and communicating clearly. I finally feel like a consultant."

That moment was a reminder of why I mentor aspiring consultants. Everyone has raw skills and expertise, but transitioning into human capital consulting requires learning the art of problem-solving, storytelling, and strategic thinking.

"You already have everything you need to succeed," I told him. *"Now you just need to sharpen how you apply it."*

Chad went on to secure a full-time consulting role specializing in Workforce Analytics, a field that perfectly matched his strengths. Watching his transformation from an uncertain MBA graduate to a confident consultant reminded me why I love this work.

Because human capital consulting is not just about helping companies; it is about empowering people to grow into the best versions of themselves.

Chapter 3: Essential Skills for Human Capital Consulting

Many professionals consider consulting but hesitate, assuming they lack the necessary background. The reality is that consulting firms do not require one rigid career trajectory—they look for people with strong problem-solving abilities, strategic thinking, and a deep understanding of business and workforce challenges. Human capital consulting, in particular, welcomes diverse backgrounds: HR, learning and development, project management, client-facing roles, business analysis, and more. The challenge is learning to *reposition* your existing skills to align with consulting demands.

To thrive in this field, you must develop and clearly articulate a set of core consulting competencies. Through research and interviews with consulting leaders, we have identified **six key skills** that are most in-demand in human capital consulting roles. The good news is you likely already have experience in some of these areas—you just need to refine those skills and learn to present them through a consulting lens.

The Six Most In-Demand Skills in Human Capital Consulting

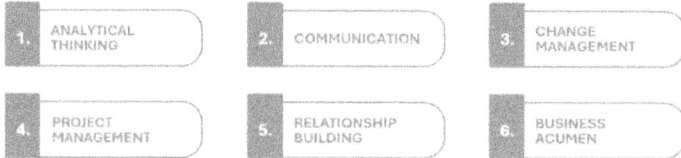

1. ANALYTICAL THINKING	2. COMMUNICATION	3. CHANGE MANAGEMENT
4. PROJECT MANAGEMENT	5. RELATIONSHIP BUILDING	6. BUSINESS ACUMEN

1) **Analytical Thinking** – *The ability to assess complex problems, extract meaningful insights from data, and develop fact-based recommendations.*

Why it matters: Consultants use analytics to diagnose talent trends (like pinpointing turnover "hotspots" or identifying gaps in workforce diversity), to predict challenges, for example, forecasting which employees might become disengaged, and to measure the outcomes of HR initiatives. In practice, this means examining data on productivity, retention, employee engagement, etc., and translating it into actionable business advice. Analytical thinking is what allows a consultant to find that "aha!" insight in a sea of data. For example, you might analyze exit data and discover that most employee turnover is happening around the two-year tenure mark—indicating a need for better career progression or mentorship around that time. That kind of insight can reshape a company's retention strategy.

Case Example: A consulting team working with a multinational retail brand noticed high turnover in one specific geographic region. The company's HR team assumed it was due to seasonal hiring cycles (a logical guess). However, by conducting a root-cause analysis, digging into exit interviews, reviewing store manager feedback, and analyzing local labor market data, the consultants discovered that inconsistent scheduling and limited career growth opportunities were the real drivers of attrition in that region. Armed with this insight, they recommended a new workforce scheduling model and a career development program. The result? The company reduced turnover in that region by 30%. This outcome shows how analytical detective work can bust myths (seasonal hiring wasn't the culprit after all) and lead to effective solutions. It also highlights a key aspect of consulting: things are not always what they seem on the surface, and a consultant's analytical lens can reveal deeper truths.

Where it applies: Virtually everywhere in human capital consulting. For instance, in Workforce Transformation projects (evaluating workforce trends and designing upskilling programs), in Change Management (identifying points of resistance or measuring change readiness), and in HR Technology implementations (conducting cost-benefit analyses for new HR systems). Nearly all consulting projects benefit from a data-driven approach. If you can demonstrate that you have used data to drive decisions in your past roles (for example, "implemented a new policy after survey data showed a need"), you are showcasing this skill.

2) **Communication** – *The ability to articulate ideas clearly, structure arguments persuasively, and present insights in a way that drives action.*

Why it matters: Consultants interact with a wide range of stakeholders: from CEOs and CFOs to frontline employees and HR staff. They often act as translators between data/strategy and the people who need to understand and act on that information. It is one thing to have a great idea, but if you can't communicate it effectively, it won't gain traction. Strong communication ensures that workforce strategies are not just understood but also embraced and implemented across the organization. This involves clarity (avoiding jargon when speaking to non-HR folks), persuasion (highlighting the benefits and addressing the "what's in it for me?" for each audience), and storytelling (making the message memorable, as discussed earlier).

Case Example: An oil and gas company underwent a major reorganization, and employees were anxious about the changes. Human capital consultants crafted a multi-channel communication strategy to explain the changes: they prepared leadership talking points and town hall presentations, created manager toolkits to guide team discussions, and published a Q&A document addressing common employee questions. This thorough communication plan led to the transition being met with 80% employee confidence in the changes (up from only 40% confidence before the communications roll-out). That's a huge swing in acceptance. It illustrates how effective communication can *double* the buy-in for a major change. People often fear what they don't understand; the consultants' strategy made the unknown feel known and showed employees the benefits of the change, which built trust and buy-in.

Where it applies: Everywhere. Some specific examples: in **Organizational Design** work, explaining a restructuring to employees and leaders requires excellent communication of the rationale and the future vision; in **Learning & Development**, delivering engaging workshops or e-learning content means being not just a subject matter expert but a good teacher and presenter; in **DEI initiatives**, facilitating sensitive discussions or trainings in a resonant way is critical.

If you have ever had to present a proposal to senior management, train a group on a new process, or roll out a policy change company-wide, you have practiced communication skills that apply to consulting. The difference is that consultants do it constantly and often in high-stakes, high-pressure settings. Honing clarity, adaptability to your audience, and professional presence (even under pressure) is very important. Later chapters will provide tips on developing an executive communication style and storytelling techniques.

3) **Change Management** – *The ability to guide organizations through transformations while minimizing resistance and disruption.*
   Why it matters: Change is hard for organizations. Whether a company is implementing new technology, merging with another company, or reimagining its culture, employees naturally worry about how the change will affect them. Consultants must anticipate these concerns and design strategies to increase adoption and reduce pushback—through training programs, transparent communication, leadership alignment, feedback loops, and so on. Effective change management drastically improves

the success rate of projects and is often the critical factor determining whether a project meets its objectives. As noted earlier, around 70% of change initiatives fail often due to people issues (resistance, poor communication, etc.). Good change management flips that dynamic—research by Prosci found that projects with excellent change management are far more likely to meet or exceed their objectives, even up to *six times* more likely (Prosci, 2018). In human capital consulting, being skilled at change management is like a superpower that amplifies the impact of your other recommendations.

Case Example: A healthcare organization introduced a new self-service HR portal for employees (for things like leave requests, viewing paystubs, etc.), but initially faced strong pushback—many employees simply weren't using it. The consultants brought in to assist took a comprehensive change management approach. They:

- **Conducted stakeholder assessments** and figured out who was resisting and why (for example, older employees felt the system was too technical, some managers feared it would create more work for them, etc.).

- **Identified adoption barriers** and discovered, for example, that the interface was not very intuitive, and many employees didn't see the personal benefit of the new system.

- **Designed a targeted training and communication plan,** and they conducted additional training workshops focused on hesitant user groups, set up drop-in help sessions, issued communications highlighting how the portal would make employees' lives easier (for example, "view your paycheck any time" convenience), and enlisted respected managers as champions to encourage their teams.

Within six months, employee usage of the portal jumped from 35% to 85%, and HR helpdesk calls dropped significantly (because people were now using the portal instead of calling HR for routine queries). Achieving that kind of turnaround in adoption in half a year is textbook change management: understanding the fears and causes of resistance, addressing them directly, equipping people to succeed with the new way, and making the case for how it benefits them. By doing so, the consultants not only improved the project outcomes but likely delivered the ROI for that new system (since its benefits were finally being realized).

Where it applies: Any project involving change—which is *most* consulting projects in some form—will value this skill. Some obvious cases: **Mergers & Acquisitions** (aligning two cultures, integrating teams and policies), **Digital Transformations** (helping employees adopt new technologies or processes, like introducing AI tools in HR), **Leadership Transitions** (coaching new leaders and helping employees adapt to leadership changes). If you have led or been part of a change initiative in your career (for example, rolling out new software, restructuring a team, implementing a new policy), think about what you did to help people through it. Did you run training sessions? Set up feedback channels? Celebrate early wins? Those are change management experiences. In consulting, you will do these things frequently, so highlighting any such experience is valuable.

4) **Project Management** – *The ability to structure, plan, and execute large-scale initiatives while managing timelines, resources, and risks.*

Why it matters: Consultants often juggle multiple tasks and workstreams, and they are expected to deliver results on time and within budget. On a typical engagement, you might have one part of the team working on data analysis, another developing training materials, another conducting stakeholder interviews—all of which have to come together by a deadline. Strong project management keeps all these moving parts on track. Moreover, many human capital projects (like implementing a company-wide training program or a new HRIS system) can impact thousands of employees. Mismanaging such projects can lead to delays, cost overruns, or even critical failures (imagine if payroll goes down because an HR system implementation missed a key step!). Consultants with good project management skills bring order to potential chaos. They use tools (project plans, Gantt charts, Agile sprints, etc.), maintain clear communication among stakeholders, and proactively mitigate risks to deliver consistently.

Case Example: A financial services firm was rolling out a new cloud-based talent management system for performance reviews and promotions. The project had fallen behind schedule due to competing business priorities—in other words, some department leaders kept delaying the implementation because they had other pressing work. Consultants were brought in to rescue the timeline. They applied Agile project management techniques, for example:

- They established an **executive steering committee** to secure buy-in from top leaders and keep them engaged. By getting senior sponsors actively involved, those leaders, in turn, made the project a priority for their teams.

- They introduced "quick-win" milestones—breaking the big project into smaller deliverables that could be completed and celebrated in shorter cycles. This showed progress and kept momentum up, proving value incrementally and motivating everyone to keep moving.

These moves got the project back on track and even completed three months *ahead* of the revised schedule. As a bonus, the firm began reaping the benefits of the new system (better performance tracking and succession planning capabilities) sooner than expected. This example shows how applying project discipline and techniques (like the Agile iterative approach and strong governance via a steering committee) can rescue or accelerate complex HR projects.

Where it applies: Common scenarios include **HR Technology implementations** (for example, a new payroll or HRIS system—with myriad tasks like data migration, testing, training users, etc.), **Workforce Analytics initiatives** (long-term projects to build data capabilities often require coordination between HR, IT, and business units), and **Employee Experience programs** (like overhauling onboarding across global offices—lots of pieces to coordinate). If you have a Project Management Professional (PMP) certification or formal project management experience, highlight it. But even if you don't have a PM title, think of times you organized a complex effort (planning a large event, coordinating a cross-department project)—that counts. Consulting firms value the ability to drive a project from start to finish.

5) **Relationship Building** – *The ability to establish trust with stakeholders, manage executive expectations, and gain buy-in for initiatives.*

Why it matters: Consulting is very much a relationship business. As the saying goes, "People buy from people they trust." A human capital consultant must quickly build rapport with clients—from HR staff to the C-suite—because you often have to influence them to take action on your recommendations (sometimes tough actions, like reorganizing a beloved team or investing in an expensive new program). Internally, if you work in a consulting firm, you also need to build relationships with colleagues and leaders to navigate the firm's culture and get staffed on the right projects. Externally, your success with a client can hinge on whether you can get a skeptical executive to open up about the real issues, or convince a busy line manager to champion your initiative with their team. Relationship building is also about empathy, understanding the human side of the business, and showing that you genuinely care about the client's people and outcomes, not just the project metrics. Clients will trust you more if they sense that your motivation is to help *them*, not just to complete a project plan.

Case Example: A consultant was brought in to design a new leadership development program for a global tech firm. Initially, a few senior executives were resistant—perhaps they felt they'd seen "yet another training program" come and go with little impact. Instead of forcing a one-size-fits-all solution, the consultant took a relational approach:

- She conducted one-on-one interviews with each executive stakeholder to understand their individual goals and concerns. This personal touch built trust and showed respect for their perspectives. For example, if one executive's priority was improving innovation in their division, the consultant noted that.

- She tailored her recommendations to align with those leadership goals. For the exec concerned about innovation, the consultant emphasized how the leadership program would foster more innovative thinking and even let that executive shape a module of the curriculum around innovation leadership. By incorporating their input, she secured that executive's buy-in.

- She identified an executive "champion," one leader who became convinced of the program's value and publicly supported it, helping to win over others. In the end, the entire leadership team actively supported and engaged in the program's rollout. Essentially, the consultant turned initial skeptics into advocates by listening and adjusting to their needs. This underscores how trust and personalization can break down barriers. In consulting, strong relationship-building can turn a lukewarm "I will tolerate this idea" into an enthusiastic "I support this initiative," which is often the difference between a paper plan and real action.

Where it applies: Everywhere, but specifically: working with **HR leaders** (consultants often partner closely with the CHRO or HR VPs—you need their trust to implement anything), with **Executives** (getting buy-in from the C-suite for big changes or investments), and even with **front-line employees** (for example, running focus groups or interviews—people will only candidly share issues if they see you as credible and on their side). If you come from a customer-facing role (like sales, account management, or an HR Business Partner role where you serve internal clients), you likely have strong relationship skills—you know how to keep people engaged, manage expectations, and build trust over time. That is gold in consulting, where stakeholder management is a daily duty.

6) Business Acumen – *The ability to connect workforce initiatives to business objectives and financial outcomes.*

Why it matters: Human capital consulting is not just about doing what's good for employees or improving HR processes in a vacuum—it is about improving the business through its people. Consulting firms want professionals who "get" the business side: revenue, costs, market pressures, competitive dynamics in the client's industry. As a consultant, you should always be able to answer the question, "How will this people initiative help the company make or save money, innovate faster, increase market share, improve customer satisfaction, or otherwise compete better?" Business acumen allows you to talk to a CFO or CEO in terms they value—like ROI, risk mitigation, and growth—when presenting your ideas. It is also crucial for prioritizing recommendations; knowing "what will potentially have the biggest strategic or financial impact" ensures you focus on changes that truly matter to the organization's success. In essence, strong business acumen turns HR from a support function into a strategic driver.

Case Example: A software company had a high attrition rate among engineers and initially assumed the issue was low pay, so their knee-jerk plan was to "throw money at the problem" by increasing salaries. The human capital consultants engaged to advise took a more data-driven, business-oriented look. After analyzing exit data and conducting interviews, they discovered compensation wasn't the top issue after all—the bigger problem was limited career progression (engineers felt

41

stuck with no clear path upward, so they left for growth opportunities elsewhere). The consultants recommended designing an internal mobility and career path framework to improve advancement opportunities. Implementing this not only reduced turnover of high performers (saving an estimated $5 million annually in recruiting and training costs), but also improved productivity by retaining experienced talent. This prevented the company from unnecessarily overspending on salaries with little effect. The consultants showed business acumen by diagnosing the *true* problem (not just accepting the easy assumption), connecting an HR intervention (career development) to financial metrics (cost savings from lower attrition), and achieving a strategic outcome (keeping top talent to maintain product development speed and customer relationships).

Where it applies: Everywhere that HR touches the business. For example: **Workforce Strategy & Planning** (ensuring the talent pipeline supports the company's long-term strategic plans, like expansion into new markets or launching new products), **HR Tech Selection** (choosing tools that not only modernize HR but also improve productivity or decision-making in the business), **Leadership Development** (training leaders to think about talent in terms of driving business results—essentially teaching line managers to be mini-HR consultants in their decision-making). If you have an MBA or experience working closely with finance or strategy teams, leverage that and speak to it. If not, you can build business acumen by deeply understanding your current industry—know how your company (or clients) make money, what their competitive landscape is, what their customers care about. In consulting interviews and jobs, you will frequently need to quantify the impact of your recommendations ("this will save $X" or "improve efficiency by Y%"). The more comfortable you are linking people initiatives to dollars and strategy, the more effective you will be as a consultant.

You might identify some skills from the above list of **six key skills** as your natural strengths and others as need to develop skills. This is normal; the key is to recognize which ones you need to work on, then actively build those skills. Perhaps you are a project management professional but need to sharpen your strategic storytelling and communication. Or maybe you are great with people (relationship building) but haven't had to analyze data much, so you will want more experience with analytics and metrics. The rest of this part is designed to help you improve each of these areas through practice, resources, and targeted actions.

Quick Self-Check: Here is a short exercise. Ask yourself the following questions (they mirror what a consulting interviewer might probe to gauge these skills):

1. **Analytical Thinking**: Can I give an example of a time I solved a work problem using data or analysis?

2. **Communication**: Can I think of a presentation or written recommendation I delivered that successfully influenced a decision?

3. **Change Management**: Have I ever helped colleagues adapt to a new way of doing things at work? What did I specifically do to ease the transition?

4. **Project Management**: Did I ever coordinate a multi-step project or initiative with multiple contributors? How did I keep it on track and ensure it met its goals?

5. **Relationship Building**: How have I built trust with a client, customer, or key stakeholder to achieve a goal? (Think of a situation where rapport and credibility made a difference.)

6. **Business Impact**: Can I connect something I did to a positive outcome for the organization's bottom line— like saving time or money, increasing revenue or customer satisfaction, or reducing risk?

If you have strong answers for some of these, great—those are stories and examples you will want to highlight on your resume and in interviews. If some are weak or you can't think of an example, note those as skills to develop moving forward.

In the next chapter, we will outline structured 90-day roadmaps for transitioning into human capital consulting from various starting points, so you can take your current experience and systematically transform it for a consulting career.

Chapter 4: Career Roadmaps

How to Transition into Human Capital Consulting: Breaking into consulting requires a structured approach, strategic positioning of your experience, and often a shift in mindset. Many professionals assume that to enter consulting they *must* have an MBA or prior consulting experience, but in reality, firms value expertise in workforce strategy, problem-solving ability, and stakeholder management just as much. The key to a successful transition is to demonstrate those advisory skills and align your previous experience with the competencies we just discussed.

This chapter provides step-by-step **90-day career transition roadmaps** tailored to various backgrounds, each designed to help you pivot into human capital consulting. We will cover roadmaps for five common profiles:

- **HR Professionals** (for example, HR Generalists, HR Business Partners, Talent Acquisition or Compensation specialists)

- **Learning & Development (L&D) Specialists**

- **Project Managers** (from any field, for example, IT or operations project managers)

- **Client-Facing Professionals** (for example, Sales, Account Managers, Customer Success roles)

- **Students/Early-Career Professionals** (recent graduates or those with 1–2 years of experience)

Each roadmap spans roughly 90 days and is broken into three phases (0–30 days, 31–60 days, 61–90 days). These aren't strict deadlines but a suggested pacing to build momentum quickly. The goal is to acquire knowledge, increase your visibility, and gain practical experience in a short time frame, making you a competitive candidate for consulting roles.

Roadmap 1: HR Professional to Human Capital Consultant

Profile Snapshot: You have experience in HR (for example, as a recruiter, HR generalist, HR business partner, compensation or benefits specialist, etc.). You understand employee relations, HR processes, and you may have led some HR initiatives internally. The challenge is shifting from a tactical/execution HR role to a strategic/advisory consulting role. The good news is you *already* speak the language of HR and have credibility on people topics—now you need to boost the consulting angle and broader business context.

Goal: Shift from being seen as an HR process executor to positioning yourself as a strategic advisor on people and workforce issues. You want to show that you can not only manage HR processes but also design people solutions that align with business strategy and influence leadership decisions.

First 30 Days – Laying the Consulting Foundation

Enroll in Business Strategy and HR Transformation courses: Strengthen your understanding of how HR initiatives connect to wider business goals. For example, consider online courses like **Human Capital Strategy** (University of Pennsylvania on Coursera) or **Consulting Essentials for HR Leaders** (Harvard Business School Online). These provide frameworks and credibility, and cover how to think strategically about HR. This will help you articulate business impact in interviews and on the job.

Study Consulting Problem-Solving Frameworks: Learn consulting tools like issue trees, hypothesis-driven analysis, and the MECE principle (we discussed MECE in **Chapter 2**). Apply them to HR scenarios to practice. For example, take a familiar HR problem (say, low employee engagement) and break it down using an issue tree: possible causes could branch into leadership factors, compensation, workload, etc. Practice structuring problems in this way. The habit of structured thinking will be invaluable.

Read Case Studies of HR Transformations: Find case studies or white papers from consulting firms (Deloitte, McKinsey, PwC, etc.) on HR transformation, culture change, M&A integration from a people perspective, etc. These show how consultants frame HR problems and solutions and often share results and ROI. Pay attention to the language and approaches used. Start incorporating that terminology in how you describe your own work (for example, if you "implemented a new onboarding process," you might reframe it as "developed a new onboarding program to accelerate time-to-productivity for new hires, improving 3-month retention by X%"). It is the same work you did, but now framed in terms of impact and metrics—which is how consultants talk.

Develop Data-Driven HR Skills: If you haven't worked much with HR analytics, now is the time. Take a course like **People Analytics** (Wharton on Coursera) to get comfortable with HR data. Also, try to get hands-on: use any HR data you have access to (even if you have to find anonymized sample data online) and practice analyzing it. For example, take a set of attrition data and see if you can find a trend—maybe turnover is highest in a certain department or at a certain employee tenure. Create a simple chart or dashboard. Being able to say, "I have used data to uncover HR insights," will set you apart.

By the end of the first 30 days, you should feel more conversant in consulting concepts and lingo. You will begin to see how to elevate your HR experience to a strategic level. Update your personal "career story" accordingly—for instance, instead of saying, "I implemented a new onboarding process," you might say, "I developed and rolled out a new onboarding program that reduced new-hire ramp-up time by 20%, improving first-year retention." It is the same achievement but now phrased in terms of business impact and outcomes.

Days 31–60 – Expanding Network & Visibility

Attend Industry Events where HR and Consulting overlap: Plug into events that focus on strategic HR topics. For example, attend a **Society for Human Resource Management (SHRM) conference session** on HR strategy or an HR Technology conference. If in-person events are hard to get to, look for webinars or virtual panels (many conferences now offer virtual attendance). These events expose you to thought leaders and potential contacts in the consulting world. They also give you talking points for interviews—for example, "At the SHRM Workforce conference, I learned how Company X used AI to improve workforce planning...". This shows you are actively learning about current trends.

Engage in Thought Leadership on LinkedIn: Start being visible online as someone interested in human capital consulting. Connect with at least 10–15 consultants who work in human capital or people advisory practices (especially at firms you are targeting). When you send a connection request, add a note like, "Hello, I am transitioning from corporate HR to consulting and found your career path inspiring—I would love to connect." Many will accept, and some may even offer a bit of advice if you politely ask. Simultaneously, build your own credibility: aim to post 2–3 short LinkedIn posts over this 30-day period about something you have learned or an insight on a workforce trend. For example, share a takeaway from one of those case studies or events: "Reading a PwC case study on upskilling—one key insight: companies saw ROI within 1 year by focusing on digital skills training..." Even if you don't get a ton of engagement, recruiters and hiring managers *will* check your LinkedIn. Seeing you write about relevant human capital topics helps set you apart as truly interested and knowledgeable.

Consider Earning a Relevant Certification: If time permits (and only if it doesn't detract from networking and skill-building), consider whether an HR or change management certification would strengthen your profile. HR folks often have credentials like SHRM-SCP or PHR; those are great but common. In consulting, something like a **Prosci Change Management certification** or a **PMP** (Project Management Professional) can be a bonus. However, remember certifications can take longer than 90 days to achieve. If you are mostly prepared (for example, you have the experience to sit for the SHRM-SCP), you might attempt it. But within a 90-day window, focus more on skills and network—don't get sidetracked studying for a test unless you are sure it is feasible and valuable.

By the end of 60 days, you should have a stronger professional network (including some new consultant contacts or HR leaders) and some visibility in the field (via your LinkedIn posts or interactions). You will also have additional industry knowledge from events and courses. All of this builds your confidence and credibility as someone who can operate at the intersection of HR and consulting.

Days 61–90 – Gaining Hands-On Consulting Experience

Develop a "Workforce Transformation" Proposal (self-directed project): This is a proactive step to simulate consulting work. Identify a company or scenario you know well—it could even be your current employer or a past one (or a well-known company in the news with a people challenge). Create a mini consulting proposal addressing a talent or workforce challenge for that organization. For instance, if your company has high turnover in a particular department, outline a consulting project to solve it: state the problem, analyze possible causes (with whatever data or observations you have), recommend initiatives (for example, mentorship program, new career paths, leadership training), and project the expected impact ("if successful, we anticipate reducing turnover by 15%, which would save approximately $200,000 in hiring costs"). Use external data or research to back up your ideas—for example, "According to a 2023 Deloitte study, companies with strong mentoring programs experience a 20% increase in retention, so we propose implementing a mentorship initiative" (Deloitte, 2018). This exercise helps solidify your learning *and* gives you something to discuss in interviews to show how you approach problems like a consultant, even if you haven't officially been one yet. You can even mention in a cover letter or interview, "Recently, I analyzed my former employer's attrition issue and put together a proposal as if I were an external consultant—and I'd love to share my findings," which is a great way to demonstrate initiative and consulting mindset.

Gain Practical Experience (Pro Bono or Internal Projects): Wherever possible, try to get a small consulting-like experience under your belt. Perhaps a local nonprofit could use HR help—there are volunteering platforms like **Taproot Foundation** or **Catchafire** that connect professionals to short-term pro bono projects. For example, you might volunteer to help a nonprofit improve their onboarding or performance review process. Alternatively, see if you can get involved in an internal project at your current job outside of your usual scope (maybe your company is forming a task force on diversity or implementing a new HR system—volunteer to participate). Even leading a "lunch-and-learn" session for your HR team on a topic you researched can count as advisory experience. The idea is to practice consulting skills in a real scenario. For instance, one HR professional volunteered with a startup to help set up their basic HR policies as they grew— she approached it like a consultant, assessing their needs and advising them, and then used that story in interviews to show her consulting approach.

Prepare for Interviews: As you near the end of 90 days, start preparing for consulting interviews (assuming you will begin applying around this time). For human capital consulting roles, you will likely face *behavioral interviews* (questions about your past experiences) and possibly *case interviews* (problem-solving exercises). Use resources like **Case in Point** by Marc Cosentino to practice case interviews, especially any HR-related cases you can find (for example, "Our company's turnover is high, what should we do?" is a potential case scenario). Also, prepare for common behavioral questions—for example, "Tell me about a time you had to convince leadership to adopt a new approach" or "Describe a challenging team project you led." Practice using the STAR method (Situation, Task, Action, Result) to structure your answers. We will go deeper into interview prep in **Part 3**, but it is not too early to start thinking about it.

Refine Your Resume and LinkedIn: By now, ensure your resume is fully "consulting-ified." Emphasize achievements with measurable results and use consulting language. For example, rather than "Handled employee onboarding," say, "Led implementation of a new onboarding program, reducing new hire time-to-productivity by 30%." Include keywords like *strategy, workforce, talent, change management, analytics,* etc., because those signal consulting fit. On LinkedIn, update your headline to something aspirational yet credible (for example, "HR Professional aspiring Human Capital Consultant | Workforce Strategy & Change Management"). Make sure your profile highlights relevant projects and any content you posted.

Where to Gain Practical Experience (Summary for HR professionals):

- Offer pro bono HR consulting to nonprofits or small businesses (via Taproot, Catchafire, or local networks).

- Join or lead an internal cross-functional project at your company that involves a people component (for example, volunteer for a new diversity initiative or a workflow improvement team).

- Take initiative to solve a problem at work beyond your usual duties, and document what you did as if it were a client engagement (this could even be something like revamping your team's process and measuring the improvement).

By the end of these 90 days, you will have significantly bolstered your profile: you will sound like a consultant, not "just an HR person." You will have evidence of proactive efforts (courses, events, volunteer projects) and perhaps even a concrete example of consulting-style work you have done. This will make you far more prepared to impress consulting firms. Your advantage is that you deeply understand HR; now, you have added a layer of strategic thinking and business language to it.

(Next, we will outline similar 90-day plans for other backgrounds— focusing on what's unique for each, while avoiding repetition of general steps already covered.)

Roadmap 2: Learning & Development (L&D) Professional to Human Capital Consultant

Profile Snapshot: You are experienced in designing and delivering training, building talent development programs, and perhaps facilitating organizational development initiatives. Your strength is understanding how people "learn and grow" and shaping programs to support that. Now, you want to pivot to consulting where you can use those skills on a broader scale—for instance, designing large-scale leadership academies for clients or advising companies on talent strategies beyond just training.

Goal: Transition from being a training program executor to a workforce transformation advisor. You will emphasize strategic thinking about learning (linking development programs to business outcomes and change efforts) and build credibility in areas that complement L&D expertise, such as analytics and change management.

30 Days: Strengthening Consulting Knowledge

Expand Knowledge Beyond Training: Enroll in courses related to change management and workforce analytics. As an L&D specialist, you likely excel at creating and delivering learning content, but consulting will demand that you also handle the *context* around training—i.e., managing the change that training is part of, and measuring its impact. For example, consider pursuing a **Prosci Change Management certification** or an online course in change management to get frameworks for handling the "people side" of change beyond just training. Likewise, take a course like **Workforce Analytics for Competitive Advantage** (Wharton) to add a data angle to your skillset. This will help you speak to ROI and metrics, which is important in consulting engagements.

Practice Structured Problem-Solving for L&D: Take a past project you did (say, creating a leadership development program) and break it down with a consulting framework. Write a one-page case study for yourself: *Situation* (for example,

"Company had poor succession pipeline"), *Complication* ("Lack of leaders was causing performance gaps and risk"), *Resolution* ("We implemented a leadership development program targeting high potentials"), and *Outcome* ("Promotions from within increased by X%, key roles were filled faster, etc."). Practicing this will help you articulate your L&D accomplishments in the concise, impact-focused manner consulting firms expect.

Study Consulting Case Studies in Talent Development: Read case studies from firms on how organizations develop their people. For instance, see if Accenture, EY, McKinsey, BCG, or Deloitte have published reports on leadership development strategies or upskilling initiatives. Observe how they talk about measuring the success of learning (you might encounter models like Kirkpatrick's four levels of training evaluation, ROI calculations, etc.). Also note the jargon: terms like "capability building," "learning culture," and "skills taxonomy." Being conversant in these terms gives you credibility with consulting interviewers and clients.

Measure Learning Impact: In your current or past L&D work, if you haven't already, try to quantify the results. For example, did a sales training program lead to improved sales numbers or product knowledge scores? Did an onboarding revamp reduce new hire turnover? Even approximate numbers help (for example, "improved training completion rates from 70% to 95% over a year"). Consultants love data. If you can show that you think in terms of outcomes and metrics, it will resonate. Try to frame at least one or two of your past L&D projects with a concrete outcome ("which led to…[business result]").

60 Days: Building External Visibility

Network with Workforce Transformation Leaders: Find events or communities specifically for L&D and talent transformation. The **Association for Talent Development (ATD) International Conference** is a big one in your field. If you can't attend, see if they have local chapter events or webinars. Also, look for meetups on "future of work" or "learning tech," which often include both corporate L&D folks and consultants. Attending these will not only teach you new trends (like VR training, microlearning, etc.) but also put you in touch with people at consulting firms who focus on learning and workforce transformation.

Engage on LinkedIn (and beyond): Join LinkedIn groups focused on Learning & Development, Talent Management, or Future of Work. Participate in discussions or comment on posts about upskilling or learning technologies. For example, if someone shares an article about "Digital Learning Trends 2025," add a thoughtful comment about how you have seen one of those trends in action. Additionally, consider writing a short article or post of your own—perhaps "3 lessons from building a leadership program" or your take on measuring training ROI. This content can catch the eye of recruiters in the talent consulting space.

Leverage Your Strength in Facilitation: One of your likely strengths is facilitating and presenting—consider offering a free webinar or workshop locally on a topic you know (maybe "Creating a Learning Culture in Small Businesses" or "Measuring the Impact of Employee Training"). This positions you as an expert and is something you can reference in interviews ("I led a workshop for local HR professionals on measuring training ROI"). It demonstrates initiative and thought leadership, which consulting firms value.

90 Days: Gaining Advisory Experience

Apply L&D Expertise in a Consulting-like Project: Try to take on a small project where you act as a consultant using your L&D skills. For example, perhaps a nonprofit or a small company you know is looking to improve their training programs—offer to assess their needs and create a plan (essentially a mini-consulting engagement). Focus on linking it to their business goals ("You want to improve customer service, so I will design a training to boost those skills and define metrics to track improvement"). This gives you a concrete consulting example outside your own employer context.

Create a "Consulting Portfolio" Artifact: Develop 1–2 tangible artifacts that show your ability to do consulting work. For an L&D professional, this could be a sample consulting proposal for a training initiative (similar to the suggestion for HR folks, but focusing on a learning solution) or a before-and-after analysis of a program you improved. Another idea: create a brief slide deck as if you were pitching an enterprise learning strategy to a client. You could base it on a well-known company's situation (for example, "Acme Corp is struggling with skill gaps—here's our proposed Learning Transformation Strategy"). Having something like this in your back pocket can be impressive if brought up during networking or interviews, showcasing your consulting presentation skills and strategic thinking.

Finalize Your Consulting Story for Interviews: As with the HR roadmap, ensure you are ready to discuss your experience in consulting-friendly terms. Prepare STAR stories that highlight times you influenced stakeholders (maybe you persuaded a stubborn manager to support a training program—that's stakeholder management), times you measured and achieved an outcome (training program results), and times you managed a tricky project (developing a program under a tight deadline, etc.). By now, you should also be actively applying to consulting roles, so tailor your resume and applications to emphasize strategic impact, not just training tasks. For example, front-load statements like "Advised senior leadership on talent development strategy leading to X outcome" rather than just "developed training content."

Your L&D background gives you a deep understanding of talent development—now you have complemented that with a broader strategic view, familiarity with change and data, and a bit of external perspective. By following this roadmap, you will present yourself as a well-rounded candidate who can both design people solutions *and* consult on the strategy behind them.

Roadmap 3: Project Management Professional to Human Capital Consulting

Profile Snapshot: You have been a Project Manager (PM), perhaps in IT, operations, or a Project Management Office (PMO), where your job is to ensure projects finish on time and on budget. You excel at coordination, risk management, and execution. Now, you want to pivot those skills into human capital consulting. While you might not be an HR expert yet, your strengths in structure and delivery are highly valued in consulting projects.

Goal: Develop enough expertise in workforce strategy and HR concepts to complement your project management prowess. Essentially, you want to pair your proven execution ability with new knowledge of people and talent issues, so you can position yourself as someone who delivers complex people-related projects effectively.

30 Days: Learning Human Capital Concepts

Study Workforce Transformation Cases: As a PM, you are used to receiving a strategy and then implementing it. To move upstream, start learning "how strategies are formed" in the talent space. Read case studies or articles about major HR transformations or organizational change projects (for example, a case about a company implementing a new performance management system or a culture change initiative). Focus on what challenges were encountered and how they were solved—often case studies will highlight, say, "we realized mid-way the training wasn't sufficient, so we adjusted." These insights connect your execution mindset with the bigger picture context.

Get Exposure to HR Tech and Planning: Familiarize yourself with major HR systems and concepts. Since many human capital projects involve implementing HR technology or processes, learn the basics of systems like Workday, SuccessFactors, or Oracle HCM (even if it is just knowing what modules like Recruiting, Payroll, Performance Management do). Also, learn key HR processes and metrics: what is workforce planning, succession planning, time-to-hire, attrition rate, engagement score, etc. Consider a LinkedIn Learning course on "HR fundamentals for non-HR managers" or "Digital HR Transformation" to build a base. This will ensure that when you are in a conversation or interview, you are not lost if acronyms like ATS (Applicant Tracking System) or D&I come up.

Learn Basics of HR Metrics: As a PM, you already think in terms of KPIs and dashboards. Extend that to HR. Learn how basic HR metrics are calculated (how do you compute turnover percentage? engagement index? cost-per-hire?). Understanding these will help you quickly grasp success measures on HR projects and speak the language of both HR and business.

Connect PM to HR with a Story: Think of a project you managed that had a significant people component or impact.

Perhaps you rolled out a new software and had to train staff (that's change management). Or you coordinated a cross-department initiative (that's breaking silos—an org development concept). Write down how you handled the people aspect: did you communicate changes carefully? Did you encounter resistance and address it? This is already human capital consulting work, framed appropriately. If you don't have a clear example, imagine how you *would* handle a hypothetical scenario (for example, "If I were managing an HR project, I would do X, Y, Z to ensure adoption"). This prepares you to discuss your relevant skills in interviews.

60 Days: Applying Project Management to Workforce Initiatives

Engage with HR Transformation Specialists: Use your network or internal company resources to learn from HR project leaders. If your company has HR Business Partners or someone leading a people-related project, take them to coffee (even a virtual coffee chat). Ask about what projects they are working on and how they approach them. Show genuine curiosity about how HR initiatives are run. Alternatively, attend webinars on topics like "Agile HR" or "Implementing HR Tech with Agile methods"—these combine your PM world with HR. Seeing how Agile or traditional PM methodologies are applied in HR contexts will likely validate that your skills are transferable and give you talking points.

Shadow or Collaborate with HR if Possible: See if you can shadow an HR project or collaborate in some way. For example, if your company is rolling out a new benefits system, volunteer to be on the project team to offer your PM expertise. Frame it as wanting to understand HR's project needs better. Even a few meetings observing how HR folks plan a rollout can be insightful. You will pick up on concerns they discuss (like employee communications and policy impacts), which you can relate to your experience.

Develop a Viewpoint on PM in HR: Consider writing a short piece or even an internal email about how project management rigor can benefit HR projects. For example, "HR transformations could benefit from Agile principle—here's why." Crafting this viewpoint forces you to articulate the value you bring. It can also serve as a discussion piece in networking: "I was thinking about how my PM background could enhance HR initiatives, especially since change is constant in that space." This signals to others (and interviewers) that you are already merging the two domains in your mind.

90 Days: Preparing for a Career Pivot

Plan and Execute a Small "People-Focused" Project: If there's an opportunity, take charge of a small initiative that involves people processes. For example, maybe your team needs a better onboarding guide—create one (project: gather info, create guide, roll it out, get feedback). Or perhaps organize a knowledge-sharing workshop series in your department (project: coordinate speakers, schedule, measure attendance/feedback). These may seem small, but they demonstrate that you can identify a people-related need and drive a project to address it—which is what human capital consultants do. Document what you did and any improvements observed.

Create a Personal Workforce Transformation Roadmap: Use your PM skills on yourself by outlining a plan for how you'd transform an HR function. Pick a hypothetical scenario like, "Our company's HR processes are outdated." Create a high-level project plan or roadmap for a transformation: perhaps phase 1: diagnostic (survey, interviews), phase 2: implement new HRIS, phase 3: training and change management, etc. It doesn't have to be detailed, but thinking this through and maybe putting it on a one-page timeline graphic can show that you understand how to structure a consulting engagement. You could even mention doing this exercise in an interview to demonstrate your proactive thinking.

Tailor Your Pitch and Resume: Now that you have built knowledge and some experience, refine how you present yourself. On your resume, highlight projects where you had a people or change component. Use phrases like "managed cross-functional team including HR and IT to deliver X" or "ensured user adoption through comprehensive training plan as part of project Y." In your cover letters or interviews, be ready to emphasize: *I bring expert project management skills, AND I have taken the initiative to learn HR strategy concepts, so I can be immediately effective in managing complex people-focused projects.* This dual value proposition is your hook.

Network into Your Target Firms: By this point, you should start reaching out to contacts (old colleagues, alumni, LinkedIn connections you made) in relevant consulting firms or practices. Request short informational chats. When you speak with them, mention how you have been preparing yourself—it shows determination. For example, "Over the last few months, I have immersed myself in HR transformation topics and even volunteered on an internal HR project, because I am serious about transitioning into people consulting."

By the end of 90 days, you will have effectively translated your project management expertise into the human capital arena. Your advantage is clear: consulting firms *need* strong execution people, so your PM skills are gold. The key was adding enough people specific context so they see you can apply those skills in a human capital consulting context. Now, you should be able to confidently convey: "I know how to drive complex projects, and I understand the unique challenges of workforce initiatives—together, that makes me an ideal human capital consultant."

Roadmap 4: Client-Facing Professional (Sales/Account Management) to Human Capital Consulting

Profile Snapshot: You might be in Sales, Business Development, Customer Success, or Account Management. You are used to interfacing with clients, understanding their needs, and delivering solutions—though currently, you are delivering products or services, not consulting advice. You have strong communication and persuasion skills, and perhaps deep industry knowledge. To pivot into consulting, you need to build more analytical and strategic muscles and show you can focus on *internal* people issues (workforce challenges) as well as you have focused on external customer issues.

Goal: Add analytical thinking and human capital knowledge to your existing strengths in communication and stakeholder management. Essentially, become a person who not only builds relationships but can also use data and frameworks to solve business problems. You want to demonstrate that you can apply your skills to improving a company's internal operations (its people and organization), not just selling to external customers.

30 Days: Understanding Workforce Transformation

Learn HR Analytics & Workforce Planning Basics: Take some introductory learning on people analytics or HR strategy. For instance, an online course like **Data-Driven HR** or **Workforce Analytics** on Coursera. As a sales or account person, you know sales metrics; now, get familiar with employee metrics. See how high employee turnover or low engagement can hurt a business (just like low customer retention would). This will help you connect the dots in conversations: for example, you might realize "high customer churn might correlate with high employee churn in customer service roles," which turns an external problem into an internal one to solve.

Develop Your Analytical Side: If your current role hasn't involved heavy analysis, practice something HR-centric to build confidence. Find a sample HR dataset (Kaggle has some HR analytics datasets available). Challenge yourself to find a story in the data: for example, do you see a trend where younger employees are leaving at higher rates, or a link between performance scores and promotion rates? You don't need to be a data scientist, but being able to say, "I recently analyzed a dataset on employee attrition to see what factors were driving it," immediately signals to consulting firms that you are not "just a talker," you can also handle data.

Identify Transferable Stories from Your Experience: Think of times in your sales/computer science career where you solved a problem using analysis or improved a process. For example, maybe a client wasn't using your product effectively, so you dug into usage data and feedback, found the issue, and recommended a solution (essentially a mini-consulting engagement!). Write a couple of these "case stories" from your experience, but frame them like a consultant would: *Problem, Analysis, Solution, Result.* For instance: "Client's software adoption was low (situation), I gathered usage data and user feedback (analysis), discovered training gaps were the issue (insight), implemented a tailored training program (solution), which increased usage by 50% (result)." This mirrors the consulting narrative style and shows problem-solving.

Familiarize with People Domain Basics: Learn basic HR concepts so you can speak that language of people. Understand terms like performance management, employee engagement, talent acquisition, succession planning, etc., and why they matter. You don't need deep expertise, just know the concepts. For example, know that "succession planning" means planning for who will fill key leadership roles in the future. You might read an "HR for beginners" guide or a few articles on "top HR challenges CEOs care about." This ensures that in an interview, you won't be thrown by terminology.

60 Days: Expanding Network and Business Acumen

Connect with HR Strategists and Consultants: Leverage LinkedIn or alumni networks to talk to people who moved from client-facing roles to consulting or HR. You may find alumni who went from, say, a sales role into an organizational development role, or consultants who focus on sales force effectiveness (which ties sales and people consulting together). When reaching out, highlight your business experience and interest in human capital consulting. People often appreciate your diverse background and can give advice on bridging the gap ("When I moved from sales to consulting, here's what I had to learn...").

Deepen Business Understanding from the Inside: As a sales professional, you likely understand revenue and customers deeply. Now, focus on internal business operations. Read up on how things like employee turnover or low morale can impact productivity and customer satisfaction—essentially linking people metrics to the bottom line. One approach: pick a company (maybe a client of yours or a well-known firm) and research a workforce challenge they had (perhaps they were in the news for a big layoff or struggle to hire enough talent). Think about it as if you were solving it. This will strengthen your ability to discuss business issues from both the external (market) and internal (people) perspectives.

Leverage Your Industry Knowledge: If you come from a specific industry (say, healthcare sales or tech account management), use that to your advantage. Consulting firms love domain knowledge. Consider writing a brief perspective: for example, "In fintech sales, I noticed clients succeed when their teams were trained continuously—companies that invest in employee development see happier clients." This links your industry knowledge with a human capital insight. You could post this on LinkedIn or simply use it as a thought exercise to mention in interviews/networking ("Having been in tech sales, I saw firsthand how internal culture affected customer outcomes, which is why I am passionate about consulting on people strategies.").

90 Days: Building Consulting Experience

Develop a Project Proposal on a Talent/Workforce Issue: Use your familiarity with business problems and craft a consulting-like proposal related to people. For example, if in your sales role, you observed high turnover in the sales team, outline a plan to address it (similar to what we did in earlier roadmaps). Or if your customers often had an issue due to their staff's skill gap, propose a workforce training initiative for such a scenario. Essentially, take a business problem you know and flip it to the people side. Write a brief proposal or slide deck.

This could even be based on a real scenario: "I noticed five of my client companies struggled with onboarding new hires quickly, so here's a 3-phase consulting solution I would offer to improve onboarding and reduce time-to-productivity." This not only helps you practice structuring a consulting solution, but it also becomes something you can share in an interview to demonstrate your approach.

Pro Bono or Side Projects: Try to get a small advisory experience. Perhaps advise a friend's small business informally on a people issue (maybe they are dealing with rapid hiring—help them outline a training plan). Or volunteer for a project at work that's not sales-related but involves improving an internal process. For example, if your company forms a committee to improve employee engagement, join it. Show that you are not just out for sales numbers, but you care about internal improvements too. This gives you a concrete story where you acted as an advisor or change agent internally.

Prepare Your Consulting Narrative: By now, you have gathered a lot of material. Update your resume to highlight achievements with internal impact: for example, "Collaborated with product and training teams to improve client onboarding, resulting in 20% faster adoption—requiring internal cross-functional leadership (demonstrating change management)." On LinkedIn, craft a headline that includes your expertise and your consulting target (for example, "Client Success Manager | Aspiring People & Strategy Consultant"). In interviews, be ready to answer the classic "Why consulting?" question with your unique story: perhaps, "In my sales career, I discovered my favorite part was analyzing my clients' challenges and helping solve them, often by improving their teams or processes. I realized I wanted to do that kind of advisory work full-time, which is why I am pursuing human capital consulting. I bring the ability to connect with stakeholders and a strong business perspective, and I have complemented that by learning analytics and HR strategy." That kind of answer shows your self-awareness and preparation.

Network Aggressively into Firms: In these final weeks, reach back out to any consulting contacts you have made. Express your readiness to interview. Perhaps ask a mentor or contact to do a mock case interview or mock behavioral interview with you, especially focusing on any perceived weaknesses (for example, if you haven't interviewed in a while or have never done a case interview, practice!). Use your sales skills to sell *yourself*—after all, that's a natural skill you have. Convey confidence that your relationship skills, combined with your new focus on analytics and strategy, will make you an effective consultant.

Your client-facing background means you are likely very strong at communication and understanding business needs— that's a huge asset. By following this roadmap, you have shown you can also crunch data and understand internal challenges. Now, you can position yourself as a consultant who not only can find the root cause of a problem but also persuade everyone to get on board with the solution—a powerful combination.

Roadmap 5: Students and Early-Career Professionals to Human Capital Consulting

Profile Snapshot: You might be a recent graduate or have 1–2 years of work experience in a field not directly related to consulting (or perhaps in a general analyst role). You are exploring consulting early in your career. You have the advantage of time and flexibility to learn, but the challenge of less work experience to draw on. You are essentially trying to break in with academic credentials and a few internships or entry-level experiences.

Goal: Rapidly build your business acumen and analytical/problem-solving skills, while demonstrating a genuine interest and foundational knowledge in human capital topics to offset your limited experience. Also, gain some relevant extracurricular exposure (like case competitions or internships) to have real examples to discuss.

30 Days: Laying the Foundation

Complete Foundational Courses: Since you are early in your career, formal learning can quickly fill gaps in your knowledge. Take courses (many are free or low-cost online) on business basics, HR fundamentals, and people analytics. For example, complete an **Introduction to HR Management** course to learn key concepts, and perhaps a general **Consulting 101** or **Strategy 101** course to learn how consultants approach problems. Also, make sure you are familiar with consulting frameworks (profitability frameworks, SWOT, etc.) by using free case prep resources or joining a consulting club if you are in university. These will train you in structured thinking.

Read, Read, Read: Devour a couple of reputable reports or books on human capital trends. Deloitte's annual **Global Human Capital Trends** report is a great comprehensive resource (for example, read the 2024 edition). It will give you insight into what CEOs and HR leaders are concerned about (for example, the skills gap, the employee experience, etc.). Learn the buzzwords and current issues: things like "the gig economy," "reskilling," and "employee well-being." This not only educates you on the content but gives you talking material for interviews ("I was interested to read in Deloitte's Trends report that 70% of CEOs are focusing on upskilling their workforce this year…").

Build Relevant Hard Skills: Make sure you are comfortable with the basic tools of the trade: Excel and PowerPoint. If you haven't done much data analysis, practice in Excel with sample data sets (there are many tutorials for creating pivot tables, basic statistical analysis, etc.). And since consultants live in slide decks, practice summarizing information in a few slides—for instance, take a topic (maybe "benefits of employee engagement") and make 3 slides that could be presented to a manager. Many new grads underestimate the importance of communicating ideas in slides—demonstrating you can do this will set you apart.

Mock Projects: If you lack real work projects, create some mock scenarios for practice. For example, write a 1-page memo or slide: "Imagine Company X hired me to improve diversity hiring—here's my approach." Use what you have learned from reading to outline steps (maybe "conduct bias audit of hiring process; implement training; set up metrics dashboard"). It doesn't have to be perfect; the point is to practice applying ideas in a structured way. This primes you for case interviews and shows initiative.

60 Days: Gaining Industry Exposure

Consulting or HR Case Competitions: Participate in any case competitions you can find, especially those focused on HR or strategy. Some organizations (like SHRM or universities) host HR case competitions where teams solve an HR-related business case. Similarly, some consulting clubs run "social impact" or business case competitions open to students. By doing a case competition, you get experience working on a consulting-style problem with a team under time pressure—plus something to put on your resume. Even if the case isn't human capital specific, doing any case comp will hone your structured thinking and teamwork, which are crucial. If there's an opportunity, join one that has a human capital slant, as that directly aligns with your goal (for instance, Deloitte has been known to run a Human Capital case competition at some universities).

Internships or Academic Projects: If you can secure even a short internship or project in an HR or consulting setting, do it. Perhaps your university's career center or a professor knows of a project (like researching for an HR professor or assisting a consultant with some analysis as an intern). Even a 4-week project over winter break can be spun into experience: for example, "assisted Prof. Smith in research on organizational change, analyzing 50 company surveys to identify common success factors." If you are already working, maybe volunteer for an internal project as mentioned in other roadmaps—but since you are early career, you might not have that opportunity yet, so focus on academic or extracurricular options.

Network, Especially with Alumni: Leverage your university network shamelessly. Reach out to alumni who work in consulting (especially those in people advisory or similar) and request informational interviews. Being a current student or recent grad is an advantage here—many alums are happy to help. Ask them what the job is like, what they recommend you do to prepare, etc. Not only will you learn, but these connections can sometimes lead to referrals. When you talk, mention the things you have been doing (courses, case comp, reading trends) to show you are serious. They might remember you when their firm is recruiting juniors.

90 Days: Building Practical Experience

Capitalize on Case Competitions or Projects: If you worked on a case competition or student consulting project, distill what you learned from it. For instance, perhaps your team had to present a solution to increase employee engagement for a fictional company. Take the feedback judges gave you and improve from it. You can even include a brief reference in interviews like, "When I tackled a case on employee engagement in a competition, I realized how critical it is to link engagement to business outcomes—we did that and ended up placing in the competition." It subtly shows experience.

Pro Bono or School Projects: If you haven't had any real-world project yet, create your own experience. For example, identify a local small business or nonprofit and offer to do a mini-project (maybe analyze their Glassdoor reviews and give recommendations, or create a new hire onboarding checklist for them). If you are still in school, perhaps you can do an independent study for credit where you effectively act as a consultant on a problem (some business programs allow this). The key is to have at least one thing that resembles consulting work that you can discuss. It is fine if it is something you initiated yourself—that entrepreneurial drive is a plus.

Network for Job Opportunities: At this point, you should be in full job-application mode for analyst or entry-level consultant positions. Use your alumni and other contacts to learn about any open roles or upcoming recruitment cycles. Attend any recruiting events (virtual info sessions, etc.) that the firms offer. When you get interviews, leverage all you have gathered: mention that you attended X webinar, read Y report, did Z competition—these things will make you stand out from other new grads who didn't put in that extra effort.

Polish Interview Skills: Practice behavioral questions (common for entry roles: teamwork, leadership examples— draw on school projects, part-time jobs, volunteer roles). Also, practice case interviews; even in human capital consulting, entry-level hires often do a case. There are case prep groups on campuses—join one if you can. Focus on structure and clear communication, which you have been developing. And remember to prepare a good answer for "Why human capital consulting?"—perhaps talking about your passion for the people side of business plus any formative experience (even something like, "In my internship, I noticed how a great manager made our team more effective, which sparked my interest in how people and organizations work...").

By the end of 90 days, you should feel like you have transformed from an interested student to an "informed and prepared" candidate. You will have a baseline of knowledge in human capital consulting topics, some practice applying consulting skills, and hopefully, a few tangible experiences to discuss. Most importantly, you will have demonstrated initiative—which goes a long way in convincing employers that you have the drive to succeed in consulting.

Following these roadmaps won't guarantee a job (there's always competition and other factors), but they significantly improve your odds. More importantly, they turn you into someone who *speaks the language* of human capital consulting and has practiced the required skills. At the end of the day, consulting firms want problem solvers who can learn and adapt quickly. By taking these steps in 90 days, you are proving exactly that about yourself.

Each roadmap shows that no matter your background—HR, L&D, PM, sales, or even new grad—there is a path to pivoting into this field. It is about leveraging what you already have and intentionally building what you are missing. In **Part 3**, we will delve into the nuts and bolts of the job search itself: how to articulate these skills on your resume, how to network your way into interviews, and how to ace those interviews when they come.

Part 3
The Consulting Job Search &
Career Acceleration

Turning Experience into Consulting: A Learning & Development Professional's First Break

"I know learning and development inside out, but consulting feels like an entirely different world. How do I make the switch?"

Daniel, a seasoned L&D specialist, had spent years designing training programs, rolling out learning platforms, and coaching leaders. But now, as he aimed to break into human capital consulting, he felt stuck.

"I have the expertise," he admitted, *"but I do not know how to position myself. Consulting firms seem to look for something different."*

I smiled, knowing this was a common challenge for professionals transitioning from corporate roles into consulting.

"You do not need to start over," I assured him. *"You just need to reframe your experience through a consulting lens."*

Together, we mapped out his strengths and built a strategy:

We shifted his mindset – Instead of thinking of his L&D experience as *delivering training*, we positioned him as someone who solved workforce capability challenges for organizations.

We revamped his resume — Instead of *"Designed leadership training programs"*, we wrote:

"Developed and implemented a leadership upskilling program that increased internal promotion rates by 30% and reduced external hiring costs by 25%."

We prepared for case interviews — He practiced structuring recommendations for consulting-style scenarios, like:

"A company is struggling with digital adoption. How would you design an upskilling program to drive employee engagement?"

Within weeks, he started getting interview calls. By the end of the month, he landed an offer.

"I finally get it," he told me. *"Consulting is not about having a different background, it is about knowing how to apply what you already know in a new way."*

Chapter 5: Understanding Consulting Firms & Job Opportunities

Breaking into human capital consulting requires not just the right skills but also knowing *where* and *how* to apply those skills. Consulting firms vary in size, focus, and culture. Understanding the landscape of potential employers will help you target your efforts.

The Top Consulting Firm Types Hiring Human Capital Consulting Professionals:

Strategy Firms (for example, McKinsey, BCG, Bain): These top-tier firms traditionally focus on overall business strategy but have expanded their talent and organization consulting practices. Strategy consultants working on human capital projects design high-level workforce models and align talent strategy with business strategy. For example, McKinsey's People & Organizational Performance team helps businesses develop leadership pipelines and organizational structures that support growth. BCG's People Strategy practice may focus on building agile organizations or rethinking HR operating models. Bain's Results Delivery® practice often specializes in change management and ensuring strategic initiatives have the right people components.

What they expect: Outstanding analytical thinking, business acumen, and the ability to tackle complex problems— your human capital expertise is valued, but you will be tested on general consulting skills intensely. Case interviews at strategy firms for human capital consulting roles will still involve rigorous structuring and quantitative analysis. They will also look for top-tier academic credentials or achievements. In return, you get exposure to C-suite projects and a variety of industries very early in your career.

Big 4 Consulting (Deloitte, PwC, EY, KPMG): These large professional services firms have dedicated human capital or people advisory practices (for example, Deloitte Human Capital, EY People Advisory Services, etc.). They provide end-to-end solutions, from high-level workforce strategy down to implementation of HR systems. A career in a Big 4 firm's human capital consulting practice often offers: wide exposure to high-profile clients across industries, structured career advancement (with clear promotion milestones from consultant to senior consultant to manager and beyond), and a fast-paced, client-driven environment that requires strong stakeholder management. Many Big 4 human capital consultants come from corporate HR or project management backgrounds, because the skills overlap (client projects might include things like implementing Workday for a client, designing a new performance management process, etc., which benefit from practical experience).

What they expect: Big 4 firms often value functional expertise and certifications (like Prosci, PMP, SHRM, etc.) in addition to consulting skills. They will expect you to be very comfortable interacting with clients early and juggling multiple projects. The recruitment process usually involves behavioral interviews and often a case or technical assessment relevant to human capital consulting (for example, how to approach a change management scenario). They also tend to hire in larger numbers, which can be an advantage in finding opportunities.

Boutique Firms (for example, Mercer, Korn Ferry, Willis Towers Watson, RHR International): These firms specialize in specific human capital areas such as compensation strategy (Mercer is well-known for that), executive leadership development and coaching (Korn Ferry, RHR), workforce analytics or assessment (WTW has analytics offerings), or culture and assessments (there are many niche players). Working at a boutique provides deeper specialization—you become an expert in that niche. The environment might be smaller teams, possibly more direct client interaction even at junior levels, and sometimes a bit less structured in terms of career path (since the firm is smaller).

What they expect: Deep interest or background in their specialty. For example, a firm like Mercer might love to hire someone with an economics background for their workforce rewards consulting. Boutiques also value self-starters because, with smaller teams, each person's contribution is highly visible. In terms of hiring, they may put more weight on specific knowledge (for example, a background in psychology for a leadership consulting boutique) and often want to see passion for that niche. The interview process may still involve case questions but is likely tailored to their focus (for example, "Design a high-level talent assessment approach for a client's succession planning" if it is a leadership boutique).

Differences Between Strategy, Big 4, and Boutique Consulting Firms: Each type has its pros and cons.

Specialization*:* Strategy firms let you touch broad organizational strategy (breadth, then you may specialize later). Big 4s cover a broad range of human capital services (from tech implementation to strategy—a mix of breadth and depth). Boutiques give you depth in one area from the start.

Client Engagement*:* Strategy firms often have you working with very senior clients on big transformations, but you might be a small cog on a large team initially. Big 4 projects can range from large implementations (where you might work with both HR and IT stakeholders) to smaller advisory projects—you will get client exposure but also lots of team support. Boutiques often put you directly in front of senior clients in their niche, since that's their selling point—high-touch expertise.

Career Progression: Big 4s typically have structured promotion paths (Analyst → Consultant → Senior Consultant → Manager → Director → Partner) with fairly regular intervals and large peer cohorts. Strategy firms also have up-or-out advancement, but the pyramid is steeper (fewer reach the top). Boutiques might have fewer formal titles and faster progression if you perform well (because there's less hierarchy) but also might not have as clear a ladder—you might wear many hats.

Understanding these nuances helps you decide where to apply.

- **If you thrive on analytical rigor and prestige**, a strategy firm might appeal.

- **If you want a balanced mix of strategy and implementation with a stable growth path**, a Big 4 human capital consulting practice is a great choice.

- **If you are passionate about a particular sub-field**, a boutique might let you become a specialist quickly.

Job Roles and Levels: In human capital consulting, entry-level roles might be called Business Analyst or Consultant (titles vary). These roles involve a lot of research, analysis (for example, crunching employee survey data, benchmarking HR practices), and preparing deliverables (PowerPoint decks, Excel models). As you progress to Senior Consultant or Manager, you take on more project management and direct client leadership—running workshops, presenting findings, etc. Senior managers and above start selling work in addition to delivering it (especially in Big 4s and boutiques). It is useful to look at job descriptions for the level you are targeting to see keywords and expectations.

Choosing the Right Firm for You: Think about your career aspirations and work style. If you prefer a structured environment with lots of training and resources, Big 4 firms invest heavily in training consultants (and have large new-hire training programs, etc.). If you want to be at the cutting edge of thought leadership, strategy firms like McKinsey/BCG produce renowned research and you will be contributing to that. If you value a tight-knit team and focused expertise (and perhaps a slightly better work-life balance, though not always), a boutique could be appealing.

Also, consider culture—even within a category, firm cultures differ. Deloitte's Human Capital practice, for instance, is very large and has a "work hard, play hard" feel with lots of camaraderie among classes of new hires. Mercer, being more specialized, might feel a bit more "corporate" and focused on subject matter expertise. Use your networking chats to get a sense of culture: ask contacts, "What kind of person succeeds here?" and listen for clues.

In summary, the human capital consulting job market offers a spectrum from huge firms to focused boutiques. Researching and understanding these will allow you to target the employers that fit you best and tailor your approach to each. Next, we will translate this understanding into your job search materials— starting with your resume and LinkedIn profile, which often form the all-important first impression.

Chapter 6: Landing Your First Consulting Role – Resume, Networking & Interviews

You have done the preparation and identified target firms—now it is time to land the job. This chapter covers how to present yourself on paper and in person: rewriting your resume for consulting, optimizing your online presence, networking effectively, and acing the interviews.

Crafting a Standout Consulting Resume: Your resume is often your ticket to an interview, especially in consulting, where recruiters may skim hundreds of resumes for key qualities. A human capital consulting resume should highlight your analytical skills, leadership/impact, and relevant people or project experience.

- **Emphasize Achievements with Impact:** Frame your experience in terms of accomplishments and outcomes, not just duties. Use action verbs and quantify results wherever possible. For example, instead of "Managed employee onboarding process," say, "Led overhaul of new hire onboarding, reducing time-to-full-productivity by 25%." Instead of "Responsible for sales in Region X," say, "Achieved 110% of sales quota by building relationships resulting in $2M revenue, demonstrating strong stakeholder management." This shows you deliver results—something consulting firms love.

- **Highlight Transferable Skills Explicitly:** If you followed the roadmaps in **Part 2**, you have gained specific skills—make sure those appear. Have a section or bullets that mention things like "Data Analysis: Analyzed employee engagement data to identify retention drivers" or "Project Management: Managed cross-functional team of 5 on timeline-driven implementation." If you earned any certifications or completed relevant courses, include them (for example, "Prosci Certified Change Practitioner," "Completed Wharton People Analytics course"). These immediately signal capability in key areas.

- **Use Consulting-Friendly Language:** Mirror the language you see in consulting job postings. Words like *analyzed, led, advised, initiated, improved, strategy, organizational, change, stakeholder, team, and impact* are good to include (truthfully). Also, consider labeling sections in a way that consultants do: for example, use "Professional Experience" rather than "Work History" and use "Education & Certifications" to call out credentials. If you have internal consulting experience (even unofficial), call it out (maybe in a summary line: "HR Specialist with experience advising leadership on workforce initiatives").

- **Keep it Clean and Structured:** Consulting resumes are typically one page (for early-career candidates) and very straightforward in format. Use consistent formatting, clear section headings, and bullet points (not long paragraphs). Recruiters spend very little time per resume; make it easy for them to pick out your key accomplishments. Avoid dense blocks of text—think of how consulting deliverables are very clear and structured; treat your resume the same way.

- **Education and Extras:** List your degrees (include strong GPAs if recent and if they are good), any honors, and relevant coursework (for example, Courses: Organizational Behavior, Strategy, Data Analysis if you took those). For early career folks, this matters. Also, list relevant skills (software like Advanced Excel, Tableau, or languages if relevant). If you have extracurricular leadership (like you were president of a university club or organized a volunteer event), include it briefly—it shows leadership and well-roundedness, which firms appreciate.

Remember, the goal of your resume is to quickly communicate: "This person has the analytical horsepower, people skills, and initiative to be a successful consultant."

Building a Professional LinkedIn and Personal Brand

In consulting, your LinkedIn profile isn't just for job searching—it is often the first place a recruiter or interviewer will look to learn more about you. Make sure it reinforces the story on your resume and showcases your interest in human capital consulting.

- **Polish Your Headline and Summary:** Your headline should be more than just your current title. Consider adding aspirational or skill-focused elements. For example: "HR Analyst | Aspiring Human Capital Consultant | Data-Driven & Change Management Focused." The summary section can be a short paragraph that connects the dots of your story—for example, "Human Resources professional with 5 years of experience driving organizational change. Passionate about aligning people strategies with business goals. Combining on-the-ground HR experience (employee relations, training programs) with analytical skills and consulting frameworks to deliver impact. Seeking to leverage this background in a human capital consulting role." This kind of summary clearly signals your intent and value proposition.

- **Showcase Key Projects and Results:** Use the Experience section to not only describe roles but also to highlight specific projects or achievements (much like the resume, but you can add a bit more narrative). You can also use the "Featured" section to link or display anything you have created—perhaps a presentation or article you wrote (maybe you posted a blog on LinkedIn about an HR topic—feature it). This visually shows thought leadership.

- **Highlight Skills and Get Endorsements/Recommen dations:** LinkedIn lets you list skills—include things like "Change Management, Data Analysis, Talent Management, Project Management, and Strategy Development." Endorsements from colleagues in those skills (even just a few) add credibility. Even better, a couple of recommendations from managers or professors that speak to your abilities can stand out—for instance, a recommendation that says, "Jane consistently provided insightful analysis on workforce metrics and was instrumental in our project's success" is gold. Don't be afraid to ask a former supervisor or mentor for a brief LinkedIn recommendation.

- **Engage Thoughtfully:** Since you have likely been reading articles and attending webinars (from **Part 2** efforts), engage with that content on LinkedIn. Share an article with a comment about why it is important, or post a short reflection on a conference you attended. This doesn't have to be daily—even a few well-considered posts or interactions over the past few months can signal to a recruiter that you are actively involved in the topics. When someone glances at your activity, they will see you talking about, say, "the importance of employee experience in digital transformation." That helps mark you as a serious candidate.

- **Professionalism and Consistency:** Ensure your profile picture is professional-looking. It doesn't need to be a suit-and-tie formal shot if that's not you, but it should be clear, well-lit, and only you in the frame, looking approachable. Also, double-check that everything on LinkedIn aligns with your resume (dates, titles, etc.). Inconsistencies can raise questions. Keep your profile free of anything too personal or unprofessional—LinkedIn isn't the place for polarizing content or casual slang, especially when job hunting.

Your personal brand online should reinforce that you are a knowledgeable, enthusiastic, and professional candidate in the human capital space. Many recruiters will form an impression of you before ever speaking, based on your online presence.

Networking into Opportunities

Networking is often what converts an application into an interview. It is especially important in consulting, where referrals and connections carry weight in a competitive process. Here's how to approach it:

- **Tap into Alumni and Common Connections:** As mentioned, start with alumni from your school or former colleagues who work at consulting firms. A friendly outreach message that establishes common ground ("We both attended XYZ University" or "I noticed you also transitioned from HR into consulting—I'd love to hear about your experience") can open doors. When you talk to them, ask about their path, what the firm looks for, and if they have advice. Often, if the conversation goes well and there's a position open, they might offer to refer you. Referred resumes often get looked at more closely. Don't directly ask for a referral first thing—focus on building rapport and learning, and if appropriate, gently express that you are applying and would appreciate any support.

- **Engage in Industry Groups (Online or Offline):** Join professional associations like SHRM or ATD and attend their local chapter events—consultants often attend these to keep up or network themselves. Join LinkedIn or Facebook groups related to consulting or HR careers. Being active and helpful in these communities can make you visible. For example, if someone asks a question about pursuing a human capital consulting career and you share your perspective, others (including perhaps a consultant or recruiter in the group) might notice and connect with you.

- **Reach Out to Recruiters:** The big consulting firms have recruiters or talent acquisition folks on LinkedIn—it is okay to politely reach out with a concise note and your interest (especially if you have applied and want to reinforce your name). Something like: "Hello, I wanted to introduce myself—I have applied for the human capital analyst position at Deloitte. I have a background in X and have been focusing on building Y skills for this role. I am really excited about the opportunity to contribute to Deloitte's Human Capital practice. I'd love to stay connected in case there are any questions about my application. Thank you for your time!" Not all will respond, but it shows proactiveness. And if you have a referral, mention that in your message (for example, "John Doe in your PAS group suggested I reach out").

- **Informational Interviews and Staying in Touch:** Not every conversation will immediately lead to a job opening. Maintain your network by keeping in touch periodically. If someone gave you advice and you followed it (say they recommended a book or course and you did it), drop them a note a few weeks later thanking them and sharing what you learned. This kind of follow-up leaves a great impression. When firms start hiring, those contacts will remember your initiative.

- **Conferences and Webinars:** In the virtual world, many conferences have networking sessions or Slack/Discord channels for attendees. Treat those like in-person networking—be curious, ask others about their roles, share your aspirations. You never know who might be in that channel—perhaps a manager at a firm who likes your enthusiasm and says, "Hey, send me your resume." Have a short "elevator pitch" ready for when someone asks about you: for example, "I am currently a data analyst with a passion for the people side of business. I have been focusing on transitioning into human capital consulting—in fact, I just completed a certification in change management—and I am excited to find an opportunity where I can help organizations with their workforce challenges." This kind of pitch is concise and memorable.

Networking can feel daunting, but remember that many people enjoy helping others, especially when there's a shared connection or story. The key is to be genuine, respectful of their time, and to show gratitude for any guidance.

Acing the Interviews: Behavioral and Case

Finally, when your networking and applications pay off, you will be interviewing. Human capital consulting interviews will test both your fit (behavioral) and your thinking (often through case questions or business scenarios).

Behavioral Interviews (Fit interviews): These assess how you handle situations, your leadership, teamwork, and motivation. Prepare specific examples from your past using the STAR method (Situation, Task, Action, Result):

- **Common Behavioral Questions:** "Tell me about a time you led a team through a challenging situation." "Give an example of a time you had to persuade someone to adopt a new approach." "Describe your greatest accomplishment at work." "Why do you want to go into consulting? Why our firm specifically?" For human capital roles, expect questions like "What interests you about working on people and change issues?" and "Tell me about a time you dealt with a difficult change at work—how did you handle it?".

- **How to Answer:** Choose examples that highlight relevant skills—for example, talk about leading a project (project management, leadership), solving a conflict in a group (relationship building, communication), or analyzing a problem (analytical thinking). Be structured: briefly set context (Situation/Task), focus on what *you* did (actions you took), and end with the positive outcome or what you learned (Result). Quantify if possible ("resulted in 15% increase in...") and emphasize what *you* personally did, even if it was a team effort (the interviewer needs to know your contribution). For the "Why consulting/why us" questions, your homework on the firm comes in handy—mention things like their specific practice areas, culture, or projects (for example, "I am drawn to PwC's People & Organization practice because of its focus on workforce analytics—I was impressed by the case study on upskilling you published. I want to be in an environment that combines data-driven insights with HR expertise, and I see that here."). And for "Why you," confidently tie your background to what the firm needs: for example, "I bring five years of hands-on HR experience and the analytical rigor I have developed through my MBA—I think that blend is ideal for tackling complex people problems as a consultant."

Case Interviews (Problem-solving interviews): Even for human capital consulting, many firms use case studies to assess how you think. These might be business cases with a human capital angle.

- **What They Look For:** Structured thinking, comfort with numbers, creativity, and the ability to communicate logic clearly. They also want to see that you can tackle ambiguous problems and break them into manageable pieces (this is where your **Chapter 2** consulting mindset practice pays off).

- **Example Case Scenarios:** "Our client's employee engagement is declining after a merger—what might be causing it and how would you address it?" or "A company is experiencing high turnover among its sales staff;

analyze the issue and recommend a solution." They could also give a more general business case (market entry or profitability) to see overall skills—don't be surprised if the case isn't purely HR. If it is general, still show awareness of the people aspect ("If they expand to a new market, they will need to consider hiring and training a new workforce there—that could be a challenge"). In an HR-focused case, be sure to connect people solutions to business outcomes ("improving engagement should raise productivity, which can boost profitability"). That demonstrates you think like a consultant who understands the business impact of human capital issues.

- **Approach:** Use a structured framework but adapt it to the question. For an engagement or turnover case, you might break it into categories like Leadership, Job Design, Rewards, Career Growth, and Work Environment (whatever makes sense). Walk the interviewer through your structure first ("I would like to examine a few areas that could affect turnover: 1) Compensation & benefits competitiveness, 2) Management/leadership issues, 3) Career development opportunities, and 4) Work conditions or culture."). Then dive into each, asking questions. Use data if provided (maybe they give you some numbers on exit survey reasons—incorporate those: "I see 40% of exiting employees cite 'lack of growth'—this points to career development as a major issue to address."). Don't forget to also suggest solutions or next steps ("To address this,

I'd recommend establishing clear career paths and a mentorship program, and perhaps conducting stay interviews with current staff to preemptively fix issues."). Even if they don't explicitly ask for recommendations until the end, laying out your thinking and possible fixes early shows a proactive approach.

- **Practice:** Before interviews, practice cases out loud, ideally with a partner or through online case prep resources. Even practicing by yourself, speak your analysis. Since human capital consulting cases might be less formulaic than, say, a market sizing, practice being flexible with structures. Also, practice basic math—sometimes you might need to calculate, for example, turnover rate or cost of turnover (for example, "turnover is 20% per year and each turnover costs $50k, so that's a $10M annual cost, quite significant"). Being able to do quick arithmetic or estimate figures helps demonstrate the "consultant mindset" that every problem has a quantitative side too.

Showcasing Your Personality and Fit: Throughout both behavioral and case portions, remember that consulting is as much about teamwork and client presence as it is about pure analysis. Be sure to:

- Listen actively to the question and your interviewer's hints or responses.

- Communicate clearly and confidently, but also collaboratively—treat the case like a dialogue, not a monologue. Ask for clarification if needed.

- Exhibit energy and enthusiasm for problem-solving—even if you are nervous, try to show that you enjoy tackling these challenges.

- Be coachable, so if the interviewer nudges you in a direction or asks a probing question, adapt and take the hint. They often want to see that you can accept and build on feedback.

- Finally, be *yourself* at your best. Consulting firms want smart people, but also people they would enjoy working long hours with. Let your genuine interest in people and consulting show. For example, during small talk or when asking your interviewer questions at the end, it is okay to let your passion show: "I have been researching a lot about organizational culture change—it is fascinating to me. What kind of culture projects have you worked on here?" Showing sincere curiosity can leave a positive impression.

By combining all these elements—a tailored resume, a strong online presence, effective networking, and solid interview performance—you significantly increase your chances of landing that first role in human capital consulting. It is a lot of work, but consider it an investment in the career you are building. The job search process itself is practice for consulting: you are essentially executing a project (with you as the product), using structured approaches, networking (client relations), and persuasive communication. Embrace it as part of your development.

Once you land the job, the journey doesn't end—it evolves. In **Part 4**, we will explore how to thrive in your new consulting role and continue accelerating your career from day one on the job.

Part 4
Thriving as a Human Capital Consultant

The First 90 Days: A New Consultant's Reality Check

"I thought landing the job was the hard part. Now I feel like I am barely keeping up."

Sophia, a newly hired human capital consultant, called me after her first two weeks on the job. She had spent months preparing for interviews, mastering case studies, and networking her way into a top consulting firm. But now, sitting in back-to-back client meetings, juggling multiple deliverables, and trying to keep up with the firm's fast-moving pace, she felt completely overwhelmed.

"Everyone speaks in frameworks and slides. I feel like I am the only one who does not know what they are doing."

I laughed, not because her struggle was funny, but because I had been there. Every consultant, no matter how experienced, has a moment of doubt when they first step into the role.

"The secret is, no one knows everything on day one," I told her. *"Consulting is about figuring things out as you go. The key is learning fast, staying adaptable, and asking the right questions."*

We built a 90-day plan to help her find her footing:

First 30 Days: Focus on listening and learning – Absorb everything: client expectations, team dynamics, and project goals. Take notes, ask thoughtful questions, and observe how senior consultants structure their work.

Days 30-60: Start adding value – Take ownership of small tasks, volunteer for research, and refine client deliverables. Find ways to make your manager's life easier—that is the fastest way to gain trust.

Days 60-90: Build confidence – Speak up in meetings, share insights, and start thinking beyond execution—what strategic recommendations can you bring to the table?

A few months later, Sophia called me again—this time, with a different tone.

"I finally feel like a consultant. I am leading client conversations, solving problems, and anticipating what my team needs before they ask. You were right, it is not about knowing everything upfront. It is about learning, adapting, and growing every day."

That is what thriving in human capital consulting looks like, not perfection, but progress, resilience, and the ability to think on your feet.

Congratulations—you have entered the world of human capital consulting! Now, the real adventure begins. Success doesn't stop at getting hired; in fact, that is just the starting line. Consulting is fast-paced, high-pressure, and continually evolving. This section will help you navigate life as a new consultant and set yourself up for long-term success.

Chapter 7: Consulting Culture – Adapting to a High-Stakes Environment

The Reality of Consulting: Many professionals enter consulting for the exciting projects, career growth, and exposure to high-profile clients—and you will get all that. But it comes with a demanding environment. Consulting often requires managing multiple priorities, meeting tight deadlines, and adapting quickly to changing client needs. The learning curve is steep, especially in the beginning.

Unlike many corporate roles where annual cycles and routine tasks are common, in consulting, priorities can shift week to week (or overnight if a client need arises). Project scope can expand, deliverable timelines can move up, and a "quick request" from a client executive can mean an all-nighter for the team. This high-stakes, high-change environment is challenging but also exhilarating for those who thrive on variety and problem-solving.

To survive and thrive, it is crucial to develop strategies for managing stress, workload, and continuous learning. The difference between a high-performing consultant and one who struggles often comes down to mindset and habits.

A common scenario: A new consultant on a human capital project recalls being asked to prepare a complete workforce analysis and executive presentation within 48 hours for a surprise client meeting. They had to prioritize effectively, tap into firm resources (perhaps templates or expert advice from colleagues), and maintain composure under pressure. By mobilizing help and focusing on what mattered most to the client, they delivered on time—earning recognition from both the client and their partners. The takeaway: success in consulting often involves being resourceful, calm under fire, and extremely good at time management.

Let's break down some key aspects of thriving in consulting culture:

Managing Multiple Projects and Expectations

It is common to be staffed on more than one engagement at a time, or to juggle client work with internal initiatives (like recruiting or thought leadership development). **Time management and organization are your lifelines.**

One useful approach consultants use is the Eisenhower Matrix (urgent vs. important). At any given moment, categorize your tasks:

- **Urgent & Important** (client deliverable due tomorrow, emergency data request) – do these first.

- **Important but Not Urgent** (developing a new framework for next month's workshop) – schedule time for these: don't neglect them or they become urgent later.

- **Urgent but Not Important** (admin tasks, scheduling meetings) – where possible, delegate or find efficient ways (maybe use firm resources or templates).

- **Neither Urgent nor Important** (some emails, low-priority tasks) – minimize these.

For example, on Monday, you might have a few tasks: finalize slides for a client meeting (urgent/important), prepare next week's training materials (important/less urgent), submit your timesheet (urgent but minor), and read a lengthy industry report (low urgency/importance right now). Focus on slides first, block time for training prep later in the week, do the timesheet quickly or automate a reminder so it is not forgotten, and skim the report for key points or save it for the weekend.

Also, use tools: whether it is the consulting staple of "to-do lists" (many consultants love OneNote, Trello, or simple notebooks) or calendar blocking to ensure you allocate time to tasks. Find a system that works for you early on.

Remember that "consultant time is managed in segments (and sometimes billed hourly)"—so be conscious of productivity. If you are working a normal full day but still drowning, speak up to your manager about prioritization. Often, they can help remove or delay something. Consulting teams know the workload is intense, and part of the culture is open communication about bandwidth. It is better to say, "I can do A and B by end of day—should we push C to tomorrow or have someone assist?" than to silently miss a deadline.

Delegation: As a junior, you might not have people *under* you to delegate to at first, but you can delegate to technology (use software to automate tasks), to peers (trading tasks based on strengths), or lean on support staff (many firms have graphics or research departments—use them for things like creating high-quality visuals or pulling data). As you become a senior consultant or manager, delegation to your team members and coaching them will be a key skill—and it starts by learning to let go of doing everything yourself.

Handling Feedback, Stakeholder Expectations, and Client Dynamics

In consulting, "feedback is constant and direct"—which is great for growth but can be jarring at first. One day you might get a document back covered in comments and redlines from a manager; a client might challenge your findings in a meeting. You need to not take it personally and iterate quickly.

When a deliverable you worked hard on comes back with heavy critique, remember, this is normal. Even veteran partners get feedback from clients that requires rework. The goal is the best outcome for the client, not getting things perfect on the first draft. Adopt a mindset of *continuous improvement*. Early on, seek feedback proactively: after a meeting or deliverable, ask your manager, "What did I do well, and what could I improve for next time?" It shows you are coachable and eager to learn. Over time, the areas of improvement will likely repeat (for example, maybe you need to be more concise in writing, or more structured in analysis)—focus on them one by one.

Client relationships can vary widely. Some clients see consultants as true partners and welcome you warmly. Others may be skeptical of your value, or even hostile ("Here come the consultants telling us what we already know."). Part of thriving is learning to adapt your communication style to different stakeholders. Some tips:

- **Map your stakeholders:** Identify who is supportive, who is neutral, and who might be resistant among the client personnel. Tailor your approach accordingly. Win over resistors by understanding their concerns—often, it is fear of change or feeling threatened. By listening and showing empathy, you can turn some skeptics into allies.

- **Adapt communication style:** Some executives love data and want the bottom line up front with numbers (analytical style). Others respond better to stories or how changes will positively affect people (narrative style). Pay attention to cues. If your client CFO keeps asking for ROI, focus your communication on numbers and business impact. If a client HR leader lights up when you talk about improving employee morale, frame your recommendations in terms of employee experience and storytelling. Recognizing preferences helps recommendations resonate (remember the example in **Chapter 2** about storytelling).

- **Manage expectations:** Under-promise and over-deliver when possible. If a client asks for something by Friday, and you think you can do it by Thursday, say Friday and delight them by delivering early. But don't consistently promise impossible deadlines to please them—it will backfire. It is better to respectfully negotiate timeline or scope than to miss a commitment. Senior consultants often say, "No client likes a surprise (unless it is a good one)." So keep them informed. If something is taking longer than expected, let them know early and explain why, with a plan to address it. They will usually understand—clients are managers of their own teams too.

Consulting often involves "influencing without authority"—you are advising, not the boss, so building trust is key. Do what you say you will. Maintain confidentiality. Show that you genuinely care about the client's success (not just delivering and leaving). Quick trust builders: asking smart questions that show you aim to understand their unique situation (not applying generic solutions), and occasionally going above and beyond (for example, sharing a relevant article or idea that isn't "billable" but adds value).

Navigating the First 90 Days in a Consulting Role

The first three months on the job often set the tone for your consulting career. Many new consultants feel overwhelmed initially—that's normal. Those who thrive focus on a few key areas early on:

1. **Building Credibility Quickly:** You want your team and clients to see you as reliable and capable. Do this by being punctual for meetings, meeting your deadlines (even small ones), and demonstrating attention to detail. Early credibility often comes from "small" things—like catching an error in data or proofreading a slide deck so the team

isn't embarrassed in front of the client. Also, speak up (respectfully) when you have a useful insight. Even if you are junior, a fresh perspective can be valuable—it shows you are thinking, not just taking orders. Over time, as you deliver good work, you will earn trust and get more responsibility.

2. **Learning the Firm's Tools and Resources:** Consulting firms have vast internal knowledge bases—frameworks, past project deliverables, research reports, etc. In your first weeks, get oriented with what's available. Maybe there's an internal wiki or portal for the human capital practice— browse it. Perhaps there are standard templates for certain analyses (a change readiness survey, a stakeholder mapping template, etc.). Using firm-standard tools will save time and also signal that you are integrating well. Also, learn the preferred software and formats (for example, the style of PowerPoint slides the firm uses, how they structure Excel models, etc.). Mastery of these tools makes you efficient and frees up brain space for the actual problem-solving.

3. **Finding Mentors and Support:** Don't do it alone. Successful consultants often cite having a mentor or "go-to" person early in their career who showed them the ropes. This could be the manager on your first project or a more experienced colleague assigned as your "buddy." Cultivate those relationships—ask them for feedback and advice. Most people remember what it was like to be new and are willing to help. Also, connect with your start class or peers—often, you learn as much from each other

(sharing tips, commiserating, brainstorming) as from formal training. There's a camaraderie in going through the intense early days together, and peers become a support network.

4. **Balancing Utilization and Professional Development:** Consulting firms track your *utilization* (time spent on client work). While you want to be fully utilized, don't neglect development. Attend the training sessions the firm offers (they usually have robust onboarding training and ongoing courses). Block some time for self-study or certification if it is supported (for instance, many firms will encourage you to get certified in an HR system or methodology relevant to your practice). This shows initiative and also builds skills you will use on projects. Yes, you may be busy 10-12 hours a day with client work, but even dedicating an hour a week to continued learning accumulates.

5. **Self-Care and Setting Boundaries (Where Possible):** The grind is real, but burnout is not the goal. Especially after the first adrenaline-filled weeks, make sure you find some sustainable rhythm. For example, if you see a gap Friday evening because a client deliverable moved, maybe leave the office a bit early to have dinner with friends or family. Take the occasional Saturday truly off to recharge (unless there's an absolute deadline). Communicate with your team about planned time off—because consulting projects can consume everything if you let them. Many firms are now much more aware of wellness; some even enforce break times or have wellness initiatives. Take

advantage of those. Remember, your long-term performance depends on not burning out. As a new consultant, you might feel pressure to be "always on," and while commitment is important, rest makes you more effective.

In summary, thriving in consulting comes down to managing yourself and your work smartly and building strong relationships. It means being proactive—in organizing your tasks, seeking feedback, and engaging with your team and clients. The learning curve never truly ends, but after a few months, you will likely find that what was once overwhelming becomes manageable, even routine. You will develop confidence that you can handle whatever the next project throws at you.

Consulting culture can be intense, but it is also incredibly rewarding. You will bond with talented colleagues through late-night work sessions, you will see your recommendations make a real impact at client organizations, and you will grow at a pace you might never have thought possible. In the next chapter, we will discuss how to continue that growth by specializing, building thought leadership, and expanding your network to propel your career to the next level.

Chapter 8: Growth and Specialization

After you have found your footing as a human capital consultant, the focus shifts from learning the basics to "charting a course for long-term success." The most successful consultants don't just execute projects—they become thought leaders, trusted advisors, and experts in their field. This chapter explores how to progress from being a competent consultant to an influential one, through specialization, thought leadership, and strategic relationship-building.

Mastering Consulting: Moving from Execution to Influence

Early in your consulting career, success is about delivering high-quality work. As you advance, success becomes about shaping engagements and even shaping client thinking. The truly effective consultants are not just solving problems handed to them; they are *anticipating* problems and guiding clients toward new insights.

One consultant at a global firm shared that in their first couple of years, they diligently completed tasks and analyses assigned to them. Their breakthrough came around year three, when they began to "proactively identify client needs" beyond the immediate project scope and suggest ways to address them. By doing so, they started conversations that led to new projects (which managers and partners certainly notice!). They shifted from being seen as just a "doer" to being seen as a *partner* in the client's success. This transition is crucial for long-term career trajectory—it is what moves you toward roles like Engagement Manager, Director, and ultimately Partner.

To make this shift, focus on three areas:

- **Specialization**
- **Thought Leadership**
- **Network/Relationship-Building**

Choosing a Specialization: The Key to Differentiation

In the first few years, you likely get exposure to a variety of project types (change management, organization design, talent strategy, HR tech implementation, etc.). While a broad foundation is valuable, as you progress, developing a *spike*—a deep expertise in a niche—becomes important.

Why specialize? It allows you to command credibility. Clients will seek you out for that expertise, and you can often charge (or be billed) at a premium for it. It also often correlates with *passion*—you will do your best work in areas you are genuinely interested in.

Common specialization areas in human capital consulting (and their appeal):

- **Organizational Design & Workforce Planning:** Advising companies on restructuring, spans and layers, role clarity, and forecasting talent needs. (Great if you enjoy structural, big-picture thinking and data analysis of orgs.)

- **Change Management & Leadership Development:** Focusing on the people side of transformations and building leadership capabilities. (Fit for those who are passionate about culture, behavior, and personal development—and like interactive work like workshops and coaching.)

- **HR Technology & People Analytics:** Implementing HRIS systems and leveraging data/AI for HR decision-making. (Appeals to the tech-savvy who like tangible systems and quantitative analysis—a growing, exciting field with lots of innovation.)

- **Diversity, Equity & Inclusion (DEI):** Developing strategies and programs for inclusive hiring, advancement, and culture. (For those driven by social impact and organizational justice—increasingly central to many orgs.)

- **Compensation & Benefits Strategy:** Designing pay structures, incentives, executive comp, and benefits programs. (Good if you have a strong analytical/financial bent and like directly tying HR to economics.)

- **Employee Experience & HR Transformation:** Holistically redesigning HR processes, improving employee lifecycle from hire to retire. (If you like thinking end-to-end and improving how HR itself operates within organizations.)

Choose a specialization that resonates with you and where market demand is strong. It is okay if this evolves—sometimes, a project ignites a new interest. But around the mid-level

(Manager or so), being "the go-to person" for something is invaluable.

How to deepen your specialization:

- Take on increasingly complex projects in that domain (volunteer for them).

- Get relevant certifications, if any (for example, a Workforce Planning certificate, Prosci for change management, CCP for compensation).

- Join professional sub-groups (like an OD Network for organization design or attend an HR tech conference).

- Write about it (we will cover in thought leadership). Perhaps publish an internal point-of-view or external article on a topic in your niche.

Specializing doesn't mean pigeonholing—you will still do varied work—but it means you have an anchor of expertise. Consultants who specialize often lead practice areas or offerings as they become senior, and they are the ones called when a tricky related issue arises.

Example: A consultant focused on workforce analytics became *the* internal guru on employee survey analysis at their firm. They leveraged that to advise big clients on measuring engagement, which then tied into larger culture strategy projects they led. Specialization was a launchpad for leadership.

Becoming a Thought Leader: Building Industry Authority

In consulting, your personal brand can greatly enhance your career. Many who advance to partnership have contributed intellectual capital: they publish, speak, and innovate frameworks. Becoming a thought leader means people in the industry recognize your name and associate it with insightful ideas in your domain.

Ways to establish thought leadership:

- **Writing for Industry Publications:** Contribute articles or whitepapers to reputable outlets. For human capital consulting, this might be journals like *HR Magazine*, *Journal of Change Management*, or your firm's own publications and blog. If writing isn't your strength, collaborate with someone who can help polish your content—it is the ideas that matter. For instance, you might publish "5 Lessons on Leading Through Digital Transformation" based on your project experiences.

- **Speaking at Conferences:** Aim to present or be on a panel at conferences such as SHRM's annual conference, ATD events, the Academy of Management (for more academic bent), or niche conferences like a Change Management Summit or HR Tech Expo. Start with smaller local events or webinars to build your speaking skills. With a few sessions under your belt, you can apply to bigger stages. Being a speaker gives you visibility and credibility beyond your firm.

- **Hosting Webinars or Roundtables:** If conferences are big steps, start by hosting a webinar (maybe your firm's marketing team is happy to set one up if you propose a good topic) or an informal roundtable with client HR leaders on a hot issue. Not only do you become associated with that topic, but you also deepen relationships by inviting clients/prospects into the discussion—a double win.

- **Posting Insights on LinkedIn or Firm Blog:** Regularly share your insights on professional networks. This doesn't have to be lengthy articles always—even short posts summarizing, say, "Key takeaways from the new diversity research and what it means for companies," can demonstrate your thought leadership. Over time, people in your network will look forward to your commentary.

- **Developing Frameworks/Tools:** Perhaps you notice recurring client problems, and you formalize a new approach or tool to solve them. For example, you create a "Hybrid Work Readiness Assessment" framework. You then apply it across projects and maybe publish it. Having a signature framework that you developed (or co-developed) can set you apart—it is something tangible that you added to the firm's intellectual arsenal.

One caution: Thought leadership efforts do take time, which may not always be billable. Often, senior leadership will support them because they enhance the firm's brand and help in business development. At mid-levels, you might do some of this on your own time (but consider it an investment in your career). Choose one channel first (writing, speaking, etc.) and build on it.

When you achieve some external recognition—for example, your article is trending or a conference invites you back—leverage that internally too. It can accelerate promotion discussions if leadership sees you elevating the firm's profile.

Thought leadership also builds confidence. The process of articulating your ideas publicly forces you to clarify your thinking, which, in turn, makes you more authoritative when advising clients.

Expanding Your Network: Relationships Drive Career Growth

As you move up, who you know (and who knows you) becomes increasingly important. Building a strong professional network both inside your firm and in the wider industry can lead to new business opportunities, partnerships, and career options.

Internally, connect beyond your immediate project teams. If your firm has different practices or offices, make an effort to meet colleagues in other areas. Often, partners in one practice have leads for projects that involve another—for example, a strategy partner has a client needing culture change help; if they know you and your expertise, they might loop you in, boosting your utilization and giving cross-practice exposure.

Find mentors at higher levels who can advocate for you in promotion discussions. Equally, mentor those below you as you become more senior—it builds your leadership skills and loyalty within the firm.

Externally, your network of clients and industry contacts is gold. Many successful consultants get a significant portion of new business from repeat clients or referrals those clients make to peers. So even after a project ends, maintain relationships:

- Periodically check in with past clients (share an article they might find useful, congratulate them on a company milestone via email or LinkedIn, etc.). This keeps you in mind for future needs.

- If some of your client contacts move to new companies (which is common), now you potentially have an "in" at a new prospective client. Reach out to say hello and learn about their new role; there may be an opportunity to work together again.

- Engage in professional associations (as mentioned) not just as a thought leader but as a networker. Join committees or volunteer roles—working side by side with other professionals (who could be potential clients or connectors) creates strong bonds.

- Don't overlook your peer network from earlier in your career—those college or MBA classmates, or fellow consultants who have since moved on to industry. As they rise into management roles at companies, they might hire consultants (and if they know you deliver, you could be the one they call). Keep in touch via occasional messages or meetups if possible.

Long-Term vs. Short-Term Networking

Some networking pays off immediately (you meet a prospect at a conference, they ask for a meeting the next week about a project need). But much of it is long-game—seeds you plant that might sprout years later. For example, the junior HR person you worked with might become an HR Director in five years, remembering how great you were to work with, and bring your firm in for a major initiative.

This points to an underlying principle: always act with integrity and professionalism, even in small interactions. The industry can be surprisingly small—reputations travel. If you build a reputation as someone who is trustworthy, helpful, and excellent at what they do, it will precede you.

Also, network within the consulting community. Other consultants (even from competing firms) can end up as colleagues or collaborators later (people switch firms). Plus, sometimes firms team up on massive projects or subcontract specialized work to each other. Having good relations industry-wide can create opportunities.

As you focus on specialization, thought leadership, and networking, a virtuous cycle kicks in: your expertise draws people to you, your public profile grows, and your network expands; in turn, those connections feed you information and opportunities that enhance your expertise further.

By the time you reach a senior role, ideally, you are seen as an *authority* in your niche with a wide network of trusted relationships. This not only makes you valuable to your firm (for business development and delivery), but it positions you for options such as partnership, or transitioning to a high-level industry role if you ever choose (many top HR executives are former consultants).

In essence, *growing* in a consulting career isn't just climbing a ladder—it is more like widening your sphere of influence and depth. You become the person who not only solves problems but also defines which problems to solve and how the industry thinks about them.

Your journey from mastering the basics to leading in the field might see you go from analyzing engagement survey data to advising a CEO on how to navigate a post-merger integration affecting tens of thousands of employees. It is a path that requires continuous learning, relationship-building, and stepping into leadership in increasing measures.

As we conclude this book, remember that the end of these chapters is truly just the beginning of your career journey. The next section will wrap up with some final thoughts and actionable next steps as you move forward.

Conclusion
Your Human Capital
Consulting Journey Begins

The Shift from Learning to Action: We have covered a lot of ground—from understanding the landscape of human capital consulting and building your skills to securing a role and thriving in the job. But reading and planning, while essential, aren't enough. The final—and most important—step is to put this knowledge into practice.

Consulting is a field of "high impact, high expectations, and high rewards." This book has aimed to provide you with a structured roadmap to break into and excel in human capital consulting. Now, it is up to you to turn those insights into tangible actions that transform your career.

Immediate Steps for Breaking into Human Capital Consulting: Let us outline some immediate next steps you can take (consider this a checklist moving forward):

Launch Your Career Transition Plan: If you are still on the journey to landing a consulting role, formalize a 90-day plan as we did in **Part 2**. Write it down and treat it as a project. For example:

- **0–30 Days:** Complete XYZ online course, update resume and LinkedIn, reach out to 5 alumni in consulting for informational chats.

- **31–60 Days:** Attend one industry event, do two practice case interviews per week, apply to at least 10 target roles.

- **61–90 Days:** Follow up with contacts, attend a consulting networking mixer, refine behavioral stories for interviews.

Track your progress each week. A written plan with specific tasks and timelines can be incredibly powerful—it turns "I hope to do this" into a project you are managing. As you achieve each milestone, you are getting closer to your goal.

Enroll in a Consulting Methodologies Course or Workshop: If you haven't already taken a formal training on consulting skills (for example, a case interview workshop, a course on consulting frameworks, or even a mini-MBA type program if you come from a non-business background), consider doing so now. Structured training can fill any remaining gaps in your toolkit and boost your confidence. Many are available online or through universities.

Gain Hands-On Experience (Case Competitions, Pro Bono, etc.): Don't wait to be in a job to practice consulting. As mentioned, case competitions or pro bono projects are excellent immediate actions. If your city has a volunteer consulting group for nonprofits (many do), join a short project—it could start next month and give you teamwork and client exposure. The idea is to *apply* your skills in a low-risk environment, which you can then talk about in interviews.

Refine Your Professional Branding: Take a fresh look at your LinkedIn profile, your elevator pitch, and even your email signature—ensure they all align to present the image of a human capital consultant (or aspiring one). For instance, if you took a certification, add it to your email signature or profile. Update your headline to reflect consulting aspirations (for example, "Human Capital Consultant | Workforce Strategy & Change Management"). These small tweaks reinforce your new professional identity to yourself and others.

Develop a Personal Consulting Pitch: Be ready to articulate your value. Write a few sentences that summarize who you are professionally, what you are skilled at, and why that's valuable in consulting. Practice saying it. You will use variants of this in networking and interviews. Having this clarity is part of turning all your prep into a compelling narrative for employers.

Expand Your Network and Visibility: Right now, pick a couple of actions to connect with the community:

- Send a message to someone you met or spoke with recently, thanking them or sharing an update ("I took your advice and enrolled in that course—it has been fantastic so far!").

- Join a professional group (online or offline) related to HR or consulting and introduce yourself.

- If you are comfortable, write a LinkedIn post summarizing something interesting you learned from this book or your preparation journey (others might find it valuable, and it subtly flags your network that you are moving into consulting). Small steps like these often lead to unexpected helpful connections.

Master Consulting Interviews and Case Studies: If you have interviews lined up (or expect to soon), double down on prep. Use resources like Case in Point or online case libraries to practice case interviews. Conduct mock behavioral interviews with friends or mentors and get feedback on your answers. The goal is to enter interviews feeling prepared for whatever question comes, rather than "I hope they don't ask X." Preparation breeds confidence, and confidence often impresses interviewers as much as the content of your answers.

Commit to Lifelong Learning and Career Acceleration: Recognize that this journey is continuous. Make a short list of things you want to keep learning or improving over the next year. Maybe it is "become proficient in advanced Excel modeling" or "gain exposure to Agile project management." Plan how you will do that—perhaps through projects or additional courses. Show your plan to mentors or even mention it in interviews ("Beyond this job, I am eager to continue developing, for example, by getting my SHRM-SCP certification in the next year."). This signals that you are proactive and growth-oriented.

This is your roadmap. The key theme is "execution, not hesitation." It is about translating intention into tangible steps.

Your Future in Consulting Begins Today

The consulting industry is constantly evolving, and organizations everywhere need professionals who can navigate workforce transformations, lead change, and align talent strategies with business success. By refining your skills and following a structured approach, you are positioning yourself as exactly the kind of problem solver companies need.

Remember that the world's top consulting firms are looking for people who not only understand the power of people in business transformation but who can also *demonstrate* it through their actions and mindset. You have built knowledge and strategies by reading this guide; now it is time to show it.

The opportunity in human capital consulting is waiting. The next step—taking what you have learned and applying it—is yours to take. Embrace it with confidence and determination.

Thank you for reading and allowing this book to be a part of your journey. I am confident that with your passion and preparation, you will make a meaningful impact in the world of human capital consulting. **Here's to your success and the high-impact career that lies ahead!**

Bonus Chapter

Introducing the BRIDGE™ Framework

If you have made it this far in the book, it means you are ready to move forward, not just in your career, but in your professional identity. You now see what human capital consulting truly involves, what skills matter most, and how your previous experience may be far more relevant than you once believed. **The question is no longer if you can pivot into consulting; it is how.**

You do not need another theory. You need a clear, actionable framework to guide your transformation.

I created the **BRIDGE™** framework to address a pattern I observed repeatedly in coaching and consulting engagements. I met professionals who had everything it takes to succeed in human capital consulting, "deep expertise, practical accomplishments, and strategic insight." They had implemented programs, influenced stakeholders, driven change, and led teams. Yet they continued to describe themselves in terms of tasks, not outcomes.

They were not lacking ability; they were lacking a structure. They needed a repeatable process to help them understand their own value, reframe their experience, and step into the advisor role with confidence.

The **BRIDGE™** framework was designed to meet that need. It provides a structured, six-stage pathway to help professionals move "from executor to advisor," to shift how they think, how they show up, and how others see them. It is not abstract theory. It is a practical model grounded in real-world experience, refined across diverse industries and career paths. If you are ready to reposition yourself, **BRIDGE™** gives you the method.

BRIDGE™ gives professionals a language for personal transformation into consulting.

It is not a set of abstract ideas; it is a practical tool to guide real career change, one stage at a time.

The six stages of the **BRIDGE™** framework enable you to move from a **practitioner to** a **strategic partner**. You **Baseline** your value, **Reframe** your story, **Interpret** challenges, **Demonstrate** your thinking, **Grow** through reflection, and **Engage** as a trusted professional.

BRIDGE™ Framework

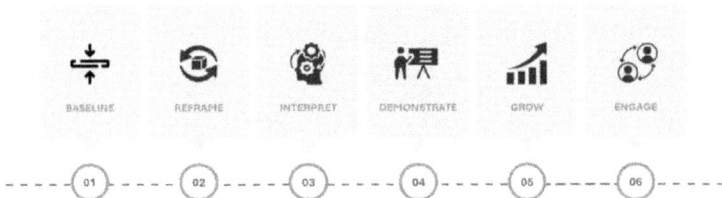

Baseline – Discover Hidden Value

What have you already done that aligns with consulting? This stage is about identifying the strategic value embedded in your past experiences—across people, processes, and performance. It is not about job titles. It is about uncovering moments where you solved problems, led change, or influenced outcomes. You begin by establishing your professional baseline.

Reframe – Shift the Narrative

This is where you begin to shift how you describe your work. Instead of saying, "I coordinated onboarding," you might say, "I designed and implemented an onboarding program that reduced new-hire attrition by 15%." The goal is to reframe your contributions in a language the business understands, "outcomes, impact, and strategic value."

Interpret – Think like a Consultant

At this stage, you begin to think like a consultant. Have you explored root cause analysis, structured problem solving, or stakeholder mapping? This phase is about interpreting challenges through a consulting lens, analyzing systems, identifying leverage points, and understanding how business problems connect to human solutions.

Demonstrate – Showcase your Thinking

Consultants communicate their thinking through deliverables, presentations, playbooks, briefs, and roadmaps. This stage is about building your portfolio, whether based on real projects or simulated work. You begin to make your approach visible, tangible, and easy for others to trust.

Grow – Commit to Growth

Repositioning yourself can be uncomfortable. This stage focuses on continuous improvement through feedback, reflection, coaching, and iteration. Growth here is not just skill-based; it is identity-based. You are building resilience and redefining how you show up professionally.

Engage – Be Seen as an Advisor

This is the stage where you take your refined story and bring it to the world. Through networking, interviews, content creation, and professional conversations, you begin to position yourself as an advisor. You are no longer just responding to opportunities; you are creating them.

What Happens When You Use the BRIDGE™ Framework

Understanding where you are in your transformation journey is often the first breakthrough. Many professionals come to this work with valuable experience, but without a clear sense of how to position it, what to build next, or where to focus. The **BRIDGE™** framework provides the structure, and the **BRIDGE™ Diagnostic Quiz** helps you identify where to begin.

I want to share a few examples of how aspiring consultants like you positioned themselves within the framework and used that insight to accelerate their development:

- **Explorer** → A mid-career HR generalist began her journey with a score in the **Explorer** range. Although she had supported large change initiatives, she had never framed her contributions in strategic terms. Focusing on the **Baseline** and **Reframe** stages, she identified several high-value projects from her past and repositioned them as advisory contributions. This shift helped her secure a secondment to her firm's transformation office.

- **Navigator** → A learning experience designer scored as a **Navigator.** She had exposure to consulting thinking but lacked structure in applying it. By working through the **Interpret** and **Demonstrate** stages, she built a robust project portfolio that highlighted her design process, stakeholder strategy, and results—leading to a successful pivot into an internal consulting role.

- **Builder** → A senior talent development lead scored as a **Builder.** She had many foundational elements in place but struggled with visibility and confidence. Through the **Grow** stage, she began seeking structured feedback, coaching, and opportunities to present. As a result, she was asked to lead a high-visibility learning strategy project.

- **Advisor** → A seasoned HR business partner scored in the **Advisor** range. She was already viewed as a leader but wanted to sharpen her strategic voice. Applying the **Engage** stage, she began publishing articles, mentoring others, and building a strong professional presence both inside and outside her organization.

BRIDGE™ Diagnostic Quiz

Discover Where You Are in Your Human Capital Consulting Journey: Take the BRIDGE™ Diagnostic Quiz to identify which stage of the **BRIDGE™** journey you are currently in and receive focused guidance for your next step. This self-assessment is designed to help you locate yourself within the **BRIDGE™** transformation pathway. Each question aligns with one of the six core stages of the framework:

- Baseline

- Reframe

- Interpret

- Demonstrate

- Grow

- Engage

Read each statement carefully and rate how true it is for you at this stage of your journey. Use the following scale to respond:

- 1 = Not true at all

- 2 = Somewhat true

- 3 = Neutral / Not sure

- 4 = Mostly true

- 5 = Absolutely true

The following statements are intended to help you assess your current alignment with each stage of the **BRIDGE™** framework. Respond as accurately as possible to reflect your present state of readiness and capability.

B – Baseline

1. I can clearly identify which aspects of my previous experience are relevant to human capital consulting.

2. I have reviewed my work history to highlight key achievements and transferable capabilities, not just job responsibilities.

R – Reframe

3. I have updated my resume and LinkedIn profile to reflect strategic outcomes and business impact.

4. I can confidently articulate my role in terms of solving business problems, rather than executing tasks.

I – Interpret

5. I understand core consulting concepts such as root cause analysis, stakeholder mapping, and issue trees.

6. I have applied consulting-style frameworks to real-world business, people, or transformation challenges.

D – Demonstrate

7. I have developed a portfolio (real or simulated) that showcases how I approach and solve complex problems.

8. I can provide examples of documents, presentations, or tools I have created that reflect strategic thinking.

G – Grow

9. I regularly seek feedback and reflect on it to strengthen my professional identity and approach.

10. I have engaged in coaching, mentorship, or peer review to support my transition into consulting.

E – Engage

11. I am actively building relationships through networking or informational conversations with professionals in human capital consulting.

12. I have begun positioning myself publicly as an emerging advisor through platforms such as LinkedIn, industry events, or thought leadership activities.

Add up your total score out of **60** and use the **Scoring Guide** below to interpret your results:

- **12–24: Explorer**

  You are at the beginning of your transition. Focus on establishing your foundation through **Baseline** and **Reframe** stages.

- **25–39: Navigator**

  You are mid-transition with some momentum. Prioritize **Interpret** and **Demonstrate** to strengthen your consulting mindset and build tangible proof of value.

- **40–49: Builder**

    You are gaining traction and beginning to show up as an advisor. Focus on deepening your **Growth** mindset and expanding your market presence.

- **50–60: Advisor**

    You are nearly ready to operate at a consulting level. Double down on visibility, thought leadership, and strategic engagement to position yourself with confidence.

Apply What You Have Learned

Based on your score, revisit the **BRIDGE™ framework** in the bonus chapter and focus on the stage where you scored lowest. Review the definition, reflect on the questions, and identify 1–2 practical actions you can take to continue building capability in that area over time.

Follow **IHCP** on LinkedIn to access tools, exercises, and updates on our upcoming courses and coaching cohorts, where you will learn to apply the **BRIDGE™** framework in practice through structured sessions that focus on real-world consulting scenarios, peer feedback, and guided reflection, designed to help you confidently transition from practitioner to advisor.

You already have the experience. Now you have the framework.

It is time to cross the bridge.

Glossary

Agile (in HR or projects): An iterative approach to project management and product development often used in software development, now applied in HR for implementing changes quickly with continuous feedback. Emphasizes adaptability and collaboration.

Analytical Thinking: The ability to logically break down problems, interpret data, and derive insights. In consulting, this often involves quantitative analysis, critical reasoning, and forming fact-based conclusions.

Business Acumen: Understanding how a business operates (revenue, costs, market dynamics) and how decisions (including people decisions) affect the company's performance. Consultants need business acumen to align HR or people solutions with overall business goals.

Change Management: A structured approach to transitioning individuals, teams, and organizations from a current state to a desired future state. In practice, it involves communication, training, stakeholder engagement, and managing resistance to ensure changes (like new systems or processes) are adopted successfully.

CHRO: Chief Human Resources Officer, the highest-ranking HR executive in an organization, responsible for overall HR strategy, including talent management, benefits, culture, etc.

Client-Facing: A role or activity involving direct interaction with clients or customers. In consulting, "client-facing" skills refer to the ability to communicate with and present to clients effectively, manage client expectations, and build strong relationships.

Deloitte Human Capital (Practice): The human capital consulting division of Deloitte (a Big 4 firm), known for providing services like organization transformation, HR tech implementation, and workforce analytics.

Diversity, Equity, and Inclusion (DEI): An organizational initiative and practice focused on ensuring a diverse workforce (variety of backgrounds), equitable opportunities and treatment for all employees, and an inclusive culture where everyone feels valued and able to contribute.

Engagement (Employee Engagement): The level of an employee's emotional commitment to an organization and its goals. High engagement is associated with higher productivity and retention. Consultants might measure and improve engagement via surveys and initiatives.

HR Business Partner (HRBP): An HR professional who works closely with a particular business unit or division to align HR strategy with business objectives. Often, an internal consultant on people matters for managers.

HR Technology (HRT or HRIS): Human Resources Technology, encompassing software systems that manage HR processes. HRIS stands for Human Resource Information System (for example, Workday, SAP SuccessFactors, Oracle HCM). Consultants might implement or optimize these systems.

Leadership Development: Programs and initiatives aimed at improving the skills and competencies of an organization's leaders or high-potential employees. Can include training programs, coaching, mentoring, job rotations, etc.

Learning & Development (L&D): The function or practice focused on improving employee capabilities and knowledge. It includes training programs, e-learning, workshops, and any learning interventions in an organization.

MECE Principle: Mutually Exclusive, Collectively Exhaustive—a framework for problem-solving that involves breaking down a problem into parts that do not overlap (mutually exclusive) and together cover everything (collectively exhaustive). Ensures structured and comprehensive analysis.

Mutually Exclusive, Collectively Exhaustive (see MECE): A method of grouping information such that each element fits into one group (no overlap) and all possible elements are included in one of the groups (no gaps).

Networking (Professional Networking): Building and maintaining professional relationships that can provide opportunities, information, and support. Includes activities like attending events, connecting on LinkedIn, and having informational meetings.

Organizational Design (Org Design): Structuring an organization's roles, hierarchy, and processes. Involves determining how teams are configured, who reports to whom, and how departments are arranged to best execute strategy and operations.

People Analytics: The use of data analysis techniques on HR and talent data to inform decision-making. Examples include analyzing what factors drive turnover or predicting which employees might become high performers. Often involves statistical analysis and data visualization.

Project Management: The practice of initiating, planning, executing, and closing a project to achieve specific goals within specific constraints (time, budget, scope). Key skills include scheduling, resource allocation, risk management, and communication. In consulting, being organized and managing tasks is a core competency.

Prosci (Change Management Certification): Prosci is a leading organization in change management research and training. They offer a well-known change management methodology (including the ADKAR model) and a certification program that many change practitioners hold.

PMP (Project Management Professional): A globally recognized certification for project managers, issued by the Project Management Institute (PMI). It signifies knowledge of project management best practices and the PMI's framework (PMBOK).

Public Speaking (in context of consulting): The act of presenting ideas or information to an audience clearly and effectively. For consultants, strong public speaking skills are important for client presentations, conference speaking, and leading workshops.

SHRM-SCP (Society for Human Resource Management – Senior Certified Professional): An advanced professional certification in HR, indicating mastery in strategic HR management. It is administered by SHRM and is recognized globally among HR practitioners.

Stakeholder: Any individual or group with an interest or stake in a project or outcome. In consulting, stakeholders often include client team members, executives, employees affected by a project, etc. Stakeholder management is managing their expectations and engagement.

STAR Method: A technique for answering behavioral interview questions by covering the Situation, Task, Action, and Result. It helps provide a structured and complete answer, focusing on what the interviewee did and what the outcome was.

Strategy Consultant (Strategy Firms): A consultant who works on high-level business strategy issues (market entry, growth strategy, etc.), often at firms like McKinsey, BCG, and Bain. In context of human capital, strategy firms also tackle talent and organizational strategy as part of their offerings.

Thought Leadership: Ideas and intellectual contributions that push forward thinking in a particular field. For a consultant, producing thought leadership (articles, frameworks, speeches) means they are helping shape the conversation in their area of expertise, not just following established ideas.

Turnover (Employee Turnover): The rate at which employees leave an organization and need to be replaced. Often measured as an annual percentage of total staff. High turnover can indicate issues with engagement, compensation, or culture, and often has costs related to recruiting and training new employees.

Workforce Planning: The process of analyzing and forecasting the needs of the workforce an organization will require to meet its objectives. It involves determining how many and what kind of employees are needed in the future, and creating plans to ensure the right talent is in place (through hiring, training, succession planning, etc.).

Work-Life Balance (in consulting context): The equilibrium between professional work and personal life. In consulting, maintaining work-life balance can be challenging due to travel and project demands. Many firms emphasize wellness and sustainable work habits to help consultants manage stress and avoid burnout.

BRIDGE™ Framework: A six-stage transformation model designed to help professionals transition from tactical roles into strategic advisory positions. The acronym stands for

Baseline, Reframe, Interpret, Demonstrate, Grow, and Engage. Each stage addresses a core element of the consulting mindset, guiding individuals to identify their transferable skills, reframe their experience, and build visibility as trusted advisors. The framework is widely used in career pivots toward human capital consulting and is supported by diagnostic tools, structured programs, and guided coaching.

Index

- Specialization (Consulting) – 14 (focusing on a niche like OD, DEI, or Analytics to become an expert and advance)

- STAR Method – 53 (structuring behavioral interview answers; also useful for self-check of experiences)

- Strategy Firms – iv (McKinsey, BCG, Bain expanding into human capital; expectations and differences vs Big4)

- Thought Leadership – iv (publishing articles, speaking, creating frameworks to become a recognized expert)

- Turnover (Employee Turnover) – xii (70% fail stat cause = resistance; solving attrition case example, cost of turnover)

- Workforce Transformation – iv (holistic changes to prepare the org. for future work trends; included in roadmaps and specialization)

(Page numbers above refer to sections or lines in this text where the term is discussed, approximated for this index since this is a fluid document.)